Library of Pastoral Care

SICK CALL

SICK CALL

A Book on the Pastoral Care of
the Physically Ill

KENNETH CHILD

LONDON
S · P · C · K
1965

First published in 1965
by S.P.C.K.
Holy Trinity Church
Marylebone Road
London N.W.1

Printed in Great Britain by
Billing and Sons Limited,
Guildford and London

Contents

Acknowledgements

Thanks are due to the following for permission to quote from copyright sources:

Darton, Longman and Todd Ltd: *Community, Church and Healing*, by R. A. Lambourne.

Macmillan and Co. Ltd and Mrs Temple: *Readings in St. John's Gospel*, by the late Archbishop William Temple.

Foreword

Every parish priest will welcome this book. Every ordinand should be made to read it. Having done so, he will want to keep it by him for reference and advice. Every candidate for a whole-time or part-time hospital chaplaincy will find it invaluable. Nurses and doctors will recognize in it the work of a priest who understands them, their skills and opportunities.

The author knows what he is talking about. Not that he writes as one who "knows all the answers". Far from it. But as a Service Chaplain, Chaplain of Guy's Hospital, and now a parish priest, he has certainly asked himself the right questions and shares with the reader in a modest and attractive way the fruits of wide experience.

The chapter headings show the comprehensive way in which the whole subject of the ministry to the sick is covered, and there is an extraordinarily happy blend of sound theory and practical advice on so many matters about which many priests need help. A useful bibliography is also included.

But what makes the book quite different from any similar production is the skill with which individual sick calls are described, the various types of priests painted in the colours in which they appear to the patients, the actual situations which all come vividly alive, because the author has great knowledge of his subject and a deep care for, and understanding of, people.

"There's an ambulance outside No. 16. I believe Mr Jones is ill." Thus begins a chapter on "Following your Sick to Hospital" that could not have been written by anyone who had not had intimate experience as a patient, a relative, and a priest. The author has been all three. And all the time Mr

Jones is a patient and under the care of the hospital chaplain and staff, you are never allowed to forget the part that Mr Jones' parish and parish priest can play in his cure.

The first chapter on "Pastoral Care" sets the tone of the whole book. And in these days when, as the writer warns us, there is a temptation to talk of "cases" rather than people, to be an amateur psychiatrist or appear in some kind of way superior to that science, it is good to read: "Why do we go to see sick people? First and foremost we go to visit them for the same reason that the shepherd goes to look at his ailing sheep. Because they are his. We go to see our sick people because they are *ours*, sick members of that part of the Body of Christ which is our pastoral responsibility."

The whole of this book abounds in common sense, quiet humour, a warm humanity that has nothing of sentimentality and everything of the compassion of Christ. It is written by a priest who owes much to finding our Lord in his vocation as a minister to the sick and whole and wants to share that experience with his brethren.

I hope that my gratitude to him will be shared by many.

✝ GEORGE GUILDFORD

Preface

I could not have written this book without the encouragement of family and friends. In particular, I should like to acknowledge the help and comments of Dr and Mrs A. E. Dossetor, the co-operation of my household, and the forbearance of my parishioners at Newmarket whom I have neglected for several weeks during this volume's gestation period.

Feast of St Lawrence 1964   KENNETH CHILD

Introduction

"Good heavens! No, no—the parson always
comes just before the undertaker."

It was a murky Thursday afternoon in November when the
new curate rang the bell at the front door of a semi-detached
house on the outskirts of a cotton town in the north of England. He had been asked by his vicar to visit a man in his late
sixties who, according to the parish grape-vine, had had a
heart attack. The man had been a sporadic worshipper at the
church and had always been most friendly and always gener-
ous with his time and his money in support of "church
things".

It seemed an eternity before anyone came to the door, but
the young priest repressed the urge to ring again because he
had seen out of the corner of his eye what even his short
experience of parish visiting had taught him were unmis-
takable signs of alertness within. The curtain of the front bay
window had moved, a face had appeared momentarily . . .
he had seen the expression on it changed from inquiry to
alarm; sounds which filtered through the letter-box, together with the hurried movements from room to room
which could be seen in distorted fashion through the
coloured glass of the front door, conveyed to the waiting
pastor the clear fact that his advent was causing something
of a commotion.

The priest tried to do what his vicar had suggested for such
occasions—to say an "Our Father . . ." as he waited for the
door to be answered. He had said the Lord's Prayer three
times and was trying to remember what the little book by
St Francis de Sales had told him that morning about

1

distractions in prayer, when the door was flung open and a rather flustered lady asked him to step inside.

"It's nice of you to come, we've never had any of the clergy before. Do come and sit down in the lounge, I'll put the kettle on—You *will* have a cup of tea, won't you?—Do you like this part of the world?" The words flowed on and it was difficult for the priest to find an opening. Finally, he did manage to blurt out that he'd heard that Mr B. was not very well and that he had come to visit him.

At that moment there was a knocking on the floor upstairs and a voice was heard, "Who is it, Margaret?" The wife went out into the hall and was heard to say in a stage whisper, "It's the new curate from the church: you know, the nice one— he's come to see you, he's heard you are not so well. Would you like him to come up?"

Before there was time to close the door and guard the ears of the now rather embarrassed but slightly amused priest, the sick man's anxious voice rumbled down the staircase: "Good heavens! No, no—the parson always comes just before the undertaker."

Much of what the reader will find in this book is based on the writer's experience both as a parish priest and as a full-time hospital chaplain and will be of little help to those who are already experienced in both these fields. In first curacies situations like the one described above can be discussed and chewed over with one's vicar or fellow-curates; in many of our theological colleges detailed instructions are given to ordinands as to how to deal with most pastoral situations.

But it has been felt that there was a need for a simple handbook for the newly ordained priest or deacon on sick visiting. There is a wealth of literature about religion and health, about psychiatry and religion, about spiritual healing —all of which ought to be read and studied by any young priest who wishes to be professionally and theologically competent. There is a danger, however, that at the beginning of a young priest's ministry he will be so bewildered by the complexities of the literature about the "ministry of healing" that he will feel that his own pastoral ministry is inadequate and inexpert in comparison with the "text-book" situations and smooth assumptions of some of the manuals which have been put into his hands. He may decide mistakenly that ministering to the sick is a specialized ministry to be left to the experts as he concentrates on running the Cub pack or editing the parish magazine, in which directions he may have outstanding gifts.

The pastoral care of the physically ill, as well as the mentally ill, is part of that pastoral care of people which is the priest's concern as described in the Ordinal. The bishop declares that it is his (the deacon's) office "to search for the sick, poor, and impotent people of the parish". He may seek for expert advice or guidance about particular cases in the same way that a general medical practitioner refers to a consultant or specialist, but his pastoral responsibility still remains. His care for that ailing and rather unattractive arthritic in that seedy house down the street should be just as assiduous as his pastoral concern for the healthy and prosperous stockbroker at the other end of the parish.

Many people may feel that all this hardly needs saying, and that all church people accept as a matter of course that the parson will visit the sick, and that they will accept quite naturally, and automatically ask for, his ministrations. One could wish that this were true, but if we are quite realistic we shall have to admit that the injunction of St James (5.14), "Is any sick among you? Let him call for the elders of the church; and let them pray over him, anointing him with oil in the name of the Lord . . ." is far from universally obeyed by even devout church people.

Nor does it seem very profitable for us to scold people for not asking for us and our ministry when they are ill. It has been known for hospital chaplains to inveigh bitterly against the inadequate teaching given by parish priests to their people about what they should do if and when they find themselves in a hospital bed. Some of us have taught year in and year out, in confirmation classes, in instructions, in sermons, and in parish magazines about the sacraments of healing and the creative use of sickness, but we still find that the feeling "It won't happen to me" takes command in the minds of our listeners or readers.

Most people learn by what happens to them as individuals, and we have to teach each person one by one about "ministering to the sick", and if this sounds to be an impossible task, then we shall have to conclude that the whole of the pastoral ministry is an impossible task. Of course, it undoubtedly would be so—if it were ours alone. But it is Christ's ministry. And that makes all the difference.

So we return to the new curate making one of his first sick visits. He meets, as he will often meet in the course of his ministry, the common idea that the visit of the priest is an unhappy omen of things to come, that the black of his garb is something akin to the "black and stripes" of the undertaker, and that he has come to administer the "last rites". He has to struggle in all that he will try to do against the *idée fixe* that the clergy are only really their natural selves when the words "sick and suffering" are sliding from their lips with alliterative sonority; and that the gaiety and strength of our Lord have little to do with the sick room or hospital ward.

This may sound like a contrived, happy ending to a chapter, but it is a fact that after many more visits and after many unorthodox attempts to establish *rapport* and friendship, the man in the room upstairs who had had a heart attack was restored to health, was prepared for confirmation, and is still, at the age of nearly 90, a communicant member of the Church.

I

Pastoral Care

> Some hope to find a skilled diplomat or a statesman,
> others a scholar or an organizer. . . . None of them is
> on the right track . . . the new Pope has before his
> mind the wonderful picture drawn by St John, in the
> words of the Saviour himself, of the Good Shepherd.[1]

At every priest's ordination in the Church of England, he is
reminded by the bishop of the high dignity and the weighty
office to which he is called—that is to say, to be a messenger,
watchman, and steward of the Lord; to teach and to pre-
monish, to feed and provide for the Lord's family; *to seek
for Christ's sheep* that are dispersed abroad. . . .

In spite of all the sentimental associations which the picture of the Good Shepherd has in the minds of many people,
the idea of the shepherd and his work must remain as the
model and the ideal for all Christian pastors and ministers
of the Gospel. Pastoral work, shepherding work, is one of the
central functions of the Christian priesthood, and we, as
priests, are bidden continually to see in Christ the Shepherd
the inspiration for our work.

Archbishop Temple reminds us that "I am the good shepherd" is more accurately translated "I am the shepherd, the
beautiful one". That is perhaps exaggerated, but we have to
remember that the word for "good" does not mean moral
uprightness nor the austerity of goodness, but its attractive-
ness. We hardly need to be reminded that it *is* possible to be
good in a particularly repelling way. In the Good Shepherd
we see the beauty of holiness and the warm humanity which
drew all men to himself.

Why do we go to see sick people? First and foremost, we go

[1] From the Coronation Day sermon of Pope John XXIII.

to visit them for the same reason that the shepherd goes to look at his ailing sheep. Because they are his. We go to see our sick people because they are *ours*, sick members of that part of the Body of Christ which is our pastoral responsibility.

This must be the background of our ministry so that we do not find ourselves being swept away by neat slogans and descriptive phrases like "the healing team" and "body, mind, and spirit" (i.e. the doctor, the psychiatrist, the priest). Of course, it is true that we are privileged to be part of a team and we shall discuss this at length in later chapters; of course, it is true that the doctor and the psychiatrist possess skills and techniques which we can never have, but we must never forget that the Good Shepherd, whom we represent and in whose name we act, is concerned with the *whole* range of healing. Theologically speaking, everything that we try to do in our ministry to the sick "over-arches" everything that others are doing. It is important that this factor is realized— otherwise it may seem to us that our task is merely to apply an additional aspirin to the medical treatment of a patient by garnishing it with a prayer.

Pastoral care, then, is concerned with the person, not with the disease, although inevitably our concern with the patient as a person involves us in consideration of his environment, the nature of his disease, and other medico-social factors. The rôle of the pastor is not that of a professional healer or a member of a healing team, but that of a shepherd: he not only cares for his sheep but he knows them and is known by them. Here is the secret of all effective pastoral work in the sick room, hospital, and parish; it is achieved through personal acquaintance—the shepherd calls his own sheep by name, he knows their qualities and their needs, and he knows how to deal with them individually.

2

Seeing ourselves as Others see us

"I've never liked the Vicar since he
ate all my grapes when I was bad."

A young theological student was taken ill and for some months was in danger of death. He still remembers vividly the stream of visitors to his bed-side during his illness and convalescence. As might be expected his visitors included many clergymen of different shapes and sizes and traditions. The procession of clerics became a topic for sly and good-humoured comment by the medical and nursing staff; "another Lambeth Conference" was how one house physician described the scene round the bed and the inevitable comment came from one Ward Sister, "Golly, *you* ought to be holy."

As the months went by, he was able to make a mental catalogue of his priestly visitors. Of course, none of us will be *quite* like any of the sketches given here, but we shall try not to err on the side of caricature and offer these clearly remembered figures as an "awful warning" for the clergyman in the sick room or hospital ward.

THE BUSY PRIEST

You hear him downstairs first of all, talking in a somewhat breathless voice. "He's just got a few minutes before rushing off to a meeting at the Bishop's and he thought he'd pop in. He'd heard that So-and-so was not so well and he really had intended to come in earlier, but what with the Gift Day and the quinquennial there hadn't been a moment. How is he?—better, he hopes. . . ."

Tension grows in the patient's mind as the torrent of

words comes nearer to the bedroom door. His first reaction is to hide beneath the bed-clothes or to pretend to be asleep; his temperature rises and his heart is thumping. He is pleased that the very busy pastor has taken the trouble to come to see him, but is fearful that he might make the man late for his appointment if he tells him all about the illness.

The next two minutes are spent in acute discomfort by both priest and patient, the priest explaining that he has to rush off to somewhere or other and the patient protesting lamely that it really does not matter. The net result of the visit amounts to a tick in the priest's diary and a good deal of secret resentment on the part of the patient.

Even if our engagement pads *are* full, we must never give the impression either deliberately or inadvertently that we are too busy to listen to our parishioners' troubles. Sometimes we shall have to sit down and listen patiently to a detailed account of all the symptoms of someone's illness, to every word of what the doctor has said; we shall have to hear about all the complicated arrangements about home helps, or the adjustments which have been made in domestic affairs; it may be that the bedclothes will be suddenly pulled down so that we may see the results of an operation or an amputation.

The wise pastor will never show by any word or change of expression that he is shocked or revolted or bored: and will remember that the sick man has "all the time in the world" even if the minister is conscious of his tightly arranged programme of visits steadily disintegrating as he listens.

"He is so busy that he wouldn't have time to listen to my problems" is a terrible condemnation of one's pastoral methods.

THE AUSTERE PRIEST

He comes into a hospital ward and makes straight for your bed without a glance to the left or right. The man on your left whispers "Good God, it's Savonarola!" and disappears behind his paperback. You have a tremendous admiration for this pastor because you know of his devoted life and the exactitude with which he carries out his priestly duties. As he shakes your hand, you are conscious of the steel in his character which you know is lamentably absent from your own.

Without much more ado, he kneels down at your bed-side, saying, "I will help you to say your prayers." He holds a crucifix on your chest and reels off some formal prayers, stands up, puts the crucifix in his pocket, shakes your hand, and walks out of the ward.

You lie still for a few moments, wondering whether the anger and embarrassment you feel are justified, whether you are really dying when you thought you were recovering, and whether that pain in your chest is your heart playing you up again or merely indigestion. Gradually you become conscious of the fact that the man in the next bed is looking at you with shy inquiry: "Blimey, that chap's a rare one—he doesn't seem to care whether you've had a leg off or had a baby."

THE "INSECURE" PRIEST

Stories about "gauche" young clergymen and their indiscretions are legion, and it would be unfair and unprofitable to retail accounts of stupidities perpetrated because of emotional immaturity. Maturity can be achieved only through experience and training in the spiritual life, but it is still true that many mistakes can be avoided if we apply rules of common sense to our ministrations.

Some pastors make the mistake of trying to make sick people "snap out of it" by making forced jokes along the lines of the "Get well" cards which people delight in sending to sick people nowadays. It is true that some patients need encouragement to cease being sorry for themselves, but to be told that the "undertakers are short of work" when one is worried to death because the "path. lab." report has indicated that you *might* have cancer hardly makes one ready to establish any kind of *rapport* with the visiting clergyman.

The young man who told the writer the woeful story about

his grapes was quite sincerely indignant because the priest who had visited him had shown much more interest—in between grapes—in the view from his window than in the boy himself.

Then there is the "professional comic" who will use the sick-room situation as an opportunity to crack jokes and to make fun of medical treatments, with many references to Dr Kildare and Ben Casey: "There was a case just like you on TV last night."

All these attitudes are a cover for the basic insecurity which the pastor feels about his rôle in the sick-room or hospital. By all means let us preserve our sense of humour, our sense of fun, not least about ourselves, but we must remember that, without being on our dignity, we have to show to people that spiritual and emotional support which those in sickness need.

THE UNTIDY PRIEST

He is a delightful person and can make interesting conversation for hours on end, but you never take him really seriously because he comes to your bed-side wearing his cycle clips and a shapeless duffle coat which has seen better days. Sometimes he has oily fingers and his hair is what the novelist calls "unruly". He is slightly vague about the hour at which he will bring you Holy Communion and is in violent contrast to the smoothly efficient and smartly attired doctor who has just left. Your heart aches because of the apparent "amateurishness" of your Church's ministers.

(One of the most beloved hospital chaplains we can remember was a shabby and badly shaved Roman Catholic priest who smoked his pipe incessantly during ward visitations and puffed clouds of smoke over his patients. There were apocryphal stories in abundance about his fumigatory exercises: rumour had it (although it was quite untrue) that he had been seen puffing his way through Sext and None. One day his pipe disappeared, never to be seen in a hospital ward again. He had found himself trying to comfort a dying man with his pipe in his mouth.)

One of the last things we should try to do is to become immaculately dressed and beautifully groomed pastors: we shall never have the money to buy our suits in Savile Row and our shirts in Piccadilly. The white-coated elegance of the Harley Street consultant is well beyond our reach. But we can be neat and clean in our attire and in our appearance: such apparently trivial things unconsciously leave the impression that the pastor intends the call to be important and respects the one whom he is visiting.

It hardly needs saying that we ought to be particularly careful about our personal hygiene. Although we may chuckle at some of the advertisements for soap or toothpaste which are designed to frighten us into the nearest chemist's shop, we ought to remember that the olfactory nerves of the sick one may be hypersensitive. Even the smell of the modest glass of sherry we had before lunch may be offensive.

THE LOUD PRIEST

We all know the clergyman who has a reputation for talking to people as if he were addressing a public meeting. He can be heard coming down the corridor or at the other end of a bus. He booms. He has got a lot to say, usually about himself or his own opinions. People look round as he goes past. Sometimes he comes into a sick-room or hospital ward. He has been known to pray or discuss one's private affairs so loudly that an acute feeling of embarrassment is felt on every side.

During sickness the nerves connected with the ears are very sensitive and even the slightest noise may annoy the patient with a headache. Those who minister to the sick must train themselves and their voices so that it is pleasant to listen to them, and they should learn to speak not unduly loud nor so soft that the patient must strain to hear him.

It is true that difficulties do sometimes arise because the

patient is hard of hearing. If the patient is very deaf but cannot lip-read, communication is best maintained by means of pencil and pad, with prayers read from a printed card (large type!) which the patient can use as the priest says them.

But the important thing is for us to learn to control our voices so that they will communicate confidence and kindness without affectation.

THE INDISCREET PRIEST

"I say, old boy, I've been talking to the Sister and she says you nearly had it last night. I hope you're feeling better. She tells me this poor chap in the next bed hasn't long to live. . . ."

And so it goes on. The ethics of his whole calling, not merely sick visiting, demand that the priest should be a man of discretion, knowing when to speak and when to keep silence.

One of the most awkward situations which can arise is when neighbours or friends of a sick person ask the priest to reveal the nature of his or her illness, especially if there is a suspicion that it may be a malignant disease. In such instances he must be guarded in his response. He may quite truthfully say that he does not know all the details and suggest that the inquirer ask a member of the family of the patient. If we acquire the reputation of being always ready to talk about other people's ailments, we shall lose the confidence of our parishioners. Many people do not want the nature of their sickness discussed by others.

It is very often better to appear to be rather "clueless" than to be known as an indiscreet cleric.

FRIENDLINESS

It was not a very happy afternoon for the bedridden student. He had been receiving nourishment through a tube which was passed through his nostrils and round the back of the throat with which the Klebbs-Loeffler Bacillus had played havoc. This method of consuming regular quantities of champagne with egg and milk had been pursued with little pleasure (he had no sense of taste) for nearly three months. A new nurse had come on duty at midday and had been given the task of feeding the patient by means of a contraption of glass and rubber tubing. She had inserted the catheter in the nostril (not without a certain amount of difficulty) and was proceeding to pour into the glass tube the mixture of egg and milk together with liberal helpings from the bottle which bore the name of *Moët et Chandon*. She was doing all this in spite of the agonized protesting of the patient who, since he was paralysed and could not speak, could only indicate his disapproval with absurd movements of his eyebrows and mouth.

The point was that he knew that the ingredients, if put into the tube in that order, would block the catheter because the champagne would curdle the milk. This he knew by experience—bitter experience. The nurse persisted nervously and the worst happened. The whole operation had to be repeated, directed rather acidly by the Ward Sister, and the atmosphere, to say the least, was a little tense.

It was at this moment that a visiting clergyman walked into the ward. The student thought, "Oh, good heavens, no, not another one", and pretended to be asleep. After a while, however, his curiosity got the better of him, and he opened his eyes to see the priest moving slowly, naturally, and with ease round the ward, talking quietly to the other men; the other patients were smiling and the tension in the ward seemed to have disappeared.

The priest came gently to the student's bed-side. He had his hands in his pockets and did not try to shake hands. ("Thoughtful of him, he must know I can't shake hands.") "Hello, I didn't like to disturb you as you seemed to be having a snooze; but it's nice to meet you. I've heard a lot about you. No! I know you can't talk, Sister told me." ("Not so bad, really; at least he seems human.") "I gather you've had a bit of a time with the old nasal feed; of course, if you *will* go in for such expensive diets. . . ." ("I should have been furious if the other parson had said that to me, but this chap seems to know how to say it. . . .") "It must be jolly uncomfortable, though, and you've certainly gone through it. Still, you're on the mend now; I know this, some of the people at my church have been wearing out their knees, praying for you." ("I suppose he must be the local Vicar and acts as Chaplain here; nice to think people have thought me worth praying about.") "Well, see you again—God bless you, and . . . we're thinking about you. . . ."

The man in the bed watched the priest move out of the ward and he noticed he was limping slightly. One day several weeks later, he asked the Ward Sister if the Chaplain had had an accident. She told him that he had had to have his leg amputated after being blown up in the First War. He was in hospital for two years. "A lot longer than you, old chum."

Friendliness—and after all, we are *supposed* to bring the friendship of Christ to people—makes us approachable. Our pastoral care for people should express itself in a friendly attitude.

That lame priest's unassuming friendliness on that afternoon certainly made its mark, in addition to improving the atmosphere of the ward.

NATURALNESS

These "horror stories" and the "success story" are really meant to underline the importance of preserving naturalness in our pastoral ministry to sick people. After all, sickness is to most people a very unnatural thing: any illness seems to them to be an unwarranted intrusion on the normality of their existence, and to encounter during an illness a ministry which is forced or insincere lends weight to the illusion that the Church has nothing to say or do in the days of illness and pain which must come to all of us.

Naturalness is one of the results of genuine compassion which is not just sympathy or pity, but an entering into the pains and ills of the patient with an understanding heart. This will involve much tedium; the priest will listen patiently to the garbled accounts of many medical histories, he may often ponder with wry admiration the curt rejoinders uttered by the giants of the Church, whose obituary notices inform us that they "did not suffer fools gladly" (as if that excused their rudeness and lack of compassion), and may be tempted to wonder if "this is what he was ordained for"— but a few minutes of meditation on chapter 10 of St John's Gospel should restore something of his vision of himself as pastor.

Compassionate understanding involves, too, the sharing of the patient's discomfort and pain in a vicarious way. We cannot share the physical pain, but we can help to bear it spiritually in our own prayers and spiritual exercises. Remembering deliberately and with understanding the ills of the people we visited the previous afternoon as we go to the altar each morning is one of the ways in which we can perform this duty.

"Yes, I know what it is like", or "I've gone through the same thing myself", can be words of great comfort, but we must beware of letting these phrases slip too easily from our lips. Otherwise we may find—with horror—that we are claiming as our own experiences we have never had in regard to major surgery or loss of limbs. For instance, the writer still remembers with acute embarrassment the moment when the words "I know what it's like" were on the tip of his tongue as he tried to minister to a man who had been blinded and had most of his face burnt away in an accident at a blast furnace.

Solomon prayed for wisdom and an understanding heart. May we, as pastors of the sick, do the same . . . and try to be men of warm humanity.

3

Physical Illness in the Parish

"There's a lot of sickness about."

The social historian will tell us of the great improvements which have been made in regard to the health of the nation; the actuary will quote statistics to prove how much greater is our expectation of life in this generation; the medical journals speak of the near-disappearance of tuberculosis and some of the infectious diseases; the obstetrician points proudly to the decline in the number of deaths in childbirth; the politician will claim credit—or some of it—for the vast amelioration of the position in regard to infantile mortality.

But sickness of one sort or another still persists. Doctors' surgeries are everlastingly crowded; more and more money is spent annually on the National Health Service and on patent medicines. Pills are now known as tablets, but consumption of them never lessens; penicillin has become as much a household word as Beechams. It may be that thousands of people recover from ailments that would have killed them a generation or two ago, but they live on only to contract more illnesses.

There are some who claim that we are becoming a nation of hypochondriacs as we watch more and more television programmes about medical matters. We know much more about the inside of a hospital than we did because of the spate of films and literature about the "dramas" that are played out there daily; we hear public discussions about doctors' and nurses' salaries, while everyday conversations are sprinkled with terms like valvotomy and hysterectomy, words which a generation ago were only looked up furtively in medical dictionaries.

But "there's still a lot of sickness about", and our parishes will go on being the fields for the exercise of our ministry to the sick, whatever the researches in medical science may bring in the way of benefits for the individual, and whatever the developments in medical ethics and medico-morals may be. It is our duty to keep abreast with contemporary developments in these fields, and to try to assess them in the light of all the Christian insights which our religion gives to us: but our duty to go and visit Mr Brown in the High Street who has just had a coronary thrombosis remains paramount.

INTELLIGENCE SYSTEM

In any well-ordered parish there is a sick list. This is used every day for the parish intercessions at the daily services, and it is the basis of the sick visiting which is done each week. The names on it are collected by the parish priest from telephone calls, from verbal messages, from the "grape-vine", from casual conversations, from requests for prayer.

Sometimes it is the practice to separate the names into "chronics" and "criticals", so that those who are old and feeble are visited regularly, and those who, say, have been taken ill suddenly with pneumonia and then recover speedily, do not have the uncomfortable experience of hearing their names read out in church when they return to give thanks, bronzed from their convalescence in Majorca, six months later.

It is quite remarkable how even the most devout worshippers will plead with their relatives and friends not to "tell the Vicar" if they are ill. We have known clergy to come into hospital as patients and to request their nurse not to let the Chaplain know. "They didn't want to be bothered." This can partly be explained by the unwillingness on the part of every one of us to admit our failure in having succumbed to one of the ills that our flesh is heir to, and by our self-centred desire to work this one out by ourselves.

But in the majority of cases our visit will be welcomed. In any case, if we miss somebody because nobody has told us, woe betide us! Six weeks later we shall meet a convalescent Mr Brown. We ask sweetly, "How are you?" Back comes the devastating reply "Better *now*, thank you". There will follow an uncomfortable few moments as we probe gently about the illness which has apparently escaped our pastoral attention. "Nearly died, you know. Hadn't you heard?" We are profuse in our explanations that nobody had told us; we are so sorry that we never went to see him. We shall be wise not to rebuke him for not sending for us, but we shall determine to improve our intelligence system.

How can this be done so that our sick list is kept up to date? One of the first duties of the P.C.C. is to keep the parish priest informed about cases of sickness. This is much more important than having a box at the back of the church marked "Messages for the Vicar", or peremptory notes in the Parish Magazine that cases of sickness should be reported immediately.

Church officers at least should erase from their minds the idea that parishioners might not like the parson to know if they are ill. It is for the priest to evaluate the information and to decide what action he ought to take in regard to any particular person.

Another system which is widely used is to have a pattern of "Street Wardens" who are responsible for letting the parish priest know about cases of sickness or bereavement in their own area. This works well so long as it is made quite clear that all "intelligence reports" are confidential, and provided that your street wardens are not notorious as "nosey parkers".

Another source of information is provided by one's friendly liaison with the general practitioner or district nurse. In small district hospitals, too, we may be allowed to look down the list of recent admissions. It is one up for the Church if—usually by chance—one arrives at the bed-side of a parishioner before the house doctor!

EVALUATING THE INTELLIGENCE

EXAMPLE 1

"Vicar, Mrs Smith is queer. The doctor's been twice to-day, the nurse is going, and I understand they've sent for Annie. I thought you ought to know." You know that Mrs Smith is in her sixties, is an occasional communicant, and is very shy. You know that she has been looking a lot older these last few months, that she is a widow living alone, and that she has two married daughters who live in another part of the country.

This is a case where the priest will go to the house as soon as possible, avoiding the hours when it is likely that the district nurse will be making the patient comfortable, or late at night when Mrs S will have "settled down for the night". You know that Mrs Smith is shy about her Church life and will not immediately ask for her priest and the ministrations of the Church.

EXAMPLE 2

"How's your husband?" The Rector is talking to people outside church after Evensong and has noticed that Mr B is not with his wife. "He's got a bad back again, Rector, and he thought he'd better rest it as he's got a heavy week ahead with the stock-taking and all that." You know that Mr B is manager of a small multiple store, has had a lot of "slipped disc" trouble, is a heavy drinker and rather over-weight. If you go to see him, he will welcome you very warmly, he'll be "glad you've come" and before you know where you are you will have a glass in your hand even if you have managed to refuse the cigar.

You will go to see him, not because of the hospitality you will receive, but because you know that he needs you as a listener. You know from your earlier visits that underneath the *bonhomie* there is a restless and unhappy Mr B, anxious and worried about a friendship that is developing with one of his floorwalkers. You may not have decided yet what advice you ought to give although he knows that you have made it quite clear that you can never condone disloyalty or unfaithfulness in marriage. But he knows you are sympathetic —and he wants to talk and talk about it. You reflect at the church door that his back will never recover until he gets his problems sorted out. Mentally you put the whole thing on the altar for the morrow—but you will go to see him during the week.

EXAMPLE 3

The telephone rings—there are the rapid pips and an agitated voice—"Father, can you come? Dad's had a haemorrhage and he's in a bad way. He keeps on saying 'Lord, have mercy upon us' and asking for you. I've rung for the doctor but he's out on his rounds and they're trying to get another one. . . ." You excuse yourself from the marriage interview and go as quickly as possible to the house. The kitchen is like a battle-field. "Dad" is on the sofa, breathing stertorously. You try to make him comfortable, and although your words may be clumsy, you attempt to bring calm to the family, whose distracted faces look to you for the healing word. "Lord have mercy" comes from the lips of the man on the sofa. "It's the priest, Dad." You think quickly that this is not the time for any formal ministry, and then you say slowly and distinctly to the sick man, "Now look, there is no need to be frightened: the doctor is coming and he'll see that you are made comfortable. You know me and I'll see that everything is all right. God is helping you and is very close to you at this moment. Lie back in his arms and let him take the weight. Now I'm going to give you his blessing." You say a blessing and let your hands gently cup his head.

The pastor's knowledge of his parish and his people will enable him, when he is experienced in the ways of folk in trouble or illness, to evaluate the mass of information that comes his way from diverse sources each day. But there are other cases about which mention should be made, and it is impossible to stress too much the importance of these.

The writer was fortunate in having for his first vicar a remarkable priest who used to say in season and out of season when discussing pastoral work, "Dear brother, no human contact is to be despised." The young priest beginning his ministry will be wise to remember this. Liturgical exactitude and knowledgeability can mean little more than having an expert knowledge of Bradshaw's Railway Guide if we forget who the liturgy is for; in much the same way our polished way of administering the Holy Communion to a devout communicant in a private nursing home has little to do with the Kingdom of God if we neglect to do anything about the little man at the shop on the corner, who has never seen the inside of a church in his life, but has just gone into hospital for prostate gland trouble, and is frightened to death.

We do not suggest for one moment that we ought to force our ministry on those who do not wish for it, but we must never give the impression that we do not go to see people in illness unless they are church-goers. "But I'm not one of yours—I'm afraid I don't belong to any Church. I think you want the people next door." We shall often meet this kind of reaction when we expand our ministry outside "normal" Church circles.

EXAMPLE 4

It was on the Feast of St Monica that the Vicar remembered he had not any cigarettes. He was on his way home to breakfast, having celebrated the Holy Mysteries in her honour: he was wondering what had happened to St Augustine's father and why the Church did not seem to hold up any happily married women for our emulation—they all seemed to be virgins or martyrs or widows. This questioning of the wisdom of Mother Church was interrupted by his about-turn to walk to the newsagent's on the corner. As he was asking for his packet of the usual, a middle-aged man came smartly into

C

the shop, swept copies of the *Guardian*, the *Daily Mirror*, and the *Sporting Life* underneath his left arm and threw a "fiver" on the counter with his right. "Good morning, Padre; nice to see you: look, here's a pound for your choirboys' outing. Cheerio!" He picked up the rest of his change and rushed out. The priest made a mental note of his choice of newspapers and the "padre" (must have been in the army) and asked the shopkeeper who the man was.

According to all the parish records he had never had any Church connections. But when the priest heard that he had been taken to hospital some weeks later he went to see him: he commended him to the hospital Chaplain, who discovered that he had been confirmed in the Army, and used to take Holy Communion to him in the hospital ward. The notable thing about this case, though, is that as a result of that man's receiving of Holy Communion two nurses on night duty in his ward asked to be prepared for confirmation.

The "chain reactions" of pastoral concern are immense.

THE OTHER SIDE OF THE PICTURE

There are those, of course, to whom the idea of a "visit" by a parson when they are in sickness is a matter for embarrassment, even of horror. We should go to them very humbly, saying that we had heard that they were unwell and that we just wanted to express our sympathy and good wishes for their recovery.

We may be told that the patient is resting, asleep, or too ill to be disturbed. We might even be asked not to call again as it might worry the patient. We shall do well not to insist on seeing the sick person but can take our leave with courtesy. The opportunity will come later—no visit is ever wasted.

Perhaps we are shown into the sick room, having had a whispered warning from the relatives, "Don't upset him, he doesn't know how poorly he is. . . ." After reassuring them, we go quietly into the room and begin the task of establishing *rapport* with the patient. If it is possible, we shake hands without man-handling the sick person. We introduce ourselves: "I'm the vicar or the priest from St So-and-so's; I heard you were not so well and I thought I'd come to see you. How are you feeling?" (It always seems rather nonsensical to say "How are you?" to somebody who is ill.)

It may be that the wife or relatives are hovering in the background or adjusting the pillows, supplying some of the answers and saying, "Oh, he's a lot better than he was—aren't you, Pop?" The onlookers are still terrified that the priest is going to say something which will frighten or disturb . . . and the priest will have to use all his accumulated wisdom in judging whether to suggest that they leave him alone with the patient or not. There can be no rule about this; sometimes it will seem right to pray with the others there, sometimes the patient will be grateful and relieved if the relatives are requested kindly to leave. It is certainly true that once a happy relationship has been established between priest, patient, and relatives (it may take two or three visits) anything is possible.

But we shall never make the mistake of thinking that our visit has been wasted if our spiritual ministrations are rejected—after all, we have not been sent for, whereas the doctor *has* been called. And they don't always follow *his* prescriptions!

BACK TO MRS SMITH

She expects us to visit her, though she is too shy to send for us. She will value our assurance that we are praying for her at church, she will accept quite naturally the suggestion that we give her a blessing at the end of her visit or pray with her. She will be slightly alarmed if we talk about bringing her Holy Communion unless we have taught constantly at church that it is a perfectly normal thing to have Communion at home, and not something left until one is in danger of death. And it is fairly certain that we shall have to do a lot of teaching about the other ministries such as the laying-on of hands or unction before all the weapons in the Church's armoury can be brought into healing use. This is where patience and pastoral skill are needed.

It may be that this is only the beginning of a long illness for Mrs Smith. Perhaps we may be able to teach her something about the offering of her pain and discomfort as an intercession for the needs of the Church and world. A wonderful old lady used to whisper to me out of her pain on a plaster bed (she had suffered multiple injuries in a car crash), "I offered this lot for S.P.G. this morning." It is doubtful if she would have understood if one had started to talk about "creative suffering". But this vale of sighs and tears, this world where "there's a lot of sickness about" will not make much sense if we deny the possibility of this constructive use of pain.

4

The Purpose of the Sick Call

"Young man, what have you got to sell?"

Sometimes at the beginning of one's ministry it is difficult to assess the "pastoral situation" when we make our first calls on people who are ill. A brisk young curate once compared *his* ministry to the sick with that of a contemporary in another parish with this slick description, "Of course, *we* take the sacraments to the sick, *they* merely take grapes." We remember one complaint about a hospital chaplain's technique which, it was said, only consisted in talking about football.

The one thing needful is to remember that we go as pastors and as ambassadors of Christ; and it is helpful to recall that ambassadors have been seen at football matches. It may be that through talking about football (or anything, really, because we may not know anything about football) we shall be able to establish that relationship which will enable us to assess more fully the pastoral situation.

If we remember our rôle and are humble enough to admit that we may not be the last word in sick visitors, it is possible for the shy and awkward, the inarticulate and stumbling young clergymen to become adept in the art of assessing what the ambassador of Christ should do in a particular set of circumstances.

A very successful shopkeeper sold his business very profitably and retired. He was able to devote all his time to his garden, and mapped out for himself a useful existence, promising himself that he would now be able to do all the things which he had wanted to do during his working life and for which he had never found time. Six months after his retirement he collapsed and found himself in bed, suffering from hyper-tension. He was told by his doctor to rest, to go carefully, to diet, to give up his pipe and whiskies and sodas, and so on. In spite of his deep disappointment he remained cheerful and brisk and accepted with a good grace his doctor's orders.

The Vicar called. He was inexperienced and had not been in the parish for long. The welcome he received was warm and sincere; he stayed for forty minutes and conversation flowed easily on every conceivable topic. At the end of the forty minutes, the priest suddenly looked at his watch, said "Good heavens! It's time for Evensong, I must fly." He shook hands and was going out of the room. "Vicar," called the man in bed, "I was a business man for forty years and I've had a lot of travellers coming into my shop. A lot of them were great talkers. I was a busy man and sometimes I had to cut the cackle and say, 'Young man, what have you got to sell?' I'm saying the same to you. You have to go now, but come back and see me to-morrow."

The versicle "O Lord, open thou our lips" seemed to have a deep meaning when that priest began to say Evensong.

When do *we* open our lips to speak of the things of God? At what stage of the interview or visit or counselling session? Is it right to speak of God or the healing weapons of the Church at all in some instances? Is it part of wise pastoral technique to keep silence altogether with some people? Christ's injunction to his disciples about their behaviour when under arrest surely applies to the pastor as he goes about his work as Christ's ambassador. . . ." Do not worry beforehand about what you will say, but when the time comes say whatever is given you to say; for it will not be you that speak, but the Holy Spirit." (Mark 13. 11, N.E.B.)

This, of course, presupposes constant meditation on the life and ministry of Christ himself. One need not be an expert in the art of mystical prayer; our aim ought to be that of the mission priest who spent most of his life on horseback or in a boat on Pacific waters: "to ponder the Scriptures so often that meditation becomes as natural as breathing".

THREE CLASSES OF PEOPLE

It is a very dangerous thing to categorize human beings, to talk about the "average" man or to speak of different grades of Christians. It may be true that in an age when computers and Gallup polls seem to be organizing our lives and aspirations, when market research workers and industrial psychologists claim to be able to predict our tastes and appetites, our individual reactions to pain and sickness can be generalized. But we still believe that the work of the Church, especially in its ministry to sick people, is an intensely personal thing incapable of being "classified".

However, the reader will perhaps bear with us if, for the purposes of this chapter, we do divide our sick folk into three classes: (a) the committed, communicant Church member; (b) the "not-so-fervent" Christian; and (c) the complete stranger with no Church connections. It is possible to criticize endlessly this sort of division, and we shall be the first to admit that it is unsatisfactory, but we shall excuse ourselves on the grounds that it conveniently fits our purpose which is to reproduce three, as it were, "tape-recorded" sessions with sick people.

(a) *The Communicant*

Man of 48 with suspected stomach ulcers

PRIEST
Hello, John! Sorry about this.

COMMUNICANT
Yes, I came to bed three days ago. I've been having these stomach pains for a long time, but it really got me down last Thursday and they had to send me home from work. Janet rang the doctor straight away; he was pretty quick in coming round, told me to stay in bed and here I am.

PRIEST
Who's your Doctor?

COMMUNICANT
Smith. Nice chap, but he doesn't tell you much.

PRIEST
Well, I know him and he's very good really. I suppose he
can't commit himself at this stage. He'd be foolish if he did.

COMMUNICANT
But it's so worrying, Vicar. I don't know how long I'm going
to be lying here and there's a big rush job on at work. The
foreman's been round twice to see what's cooking. And
Janet's worried to death. The eldest girl ought to be doing
more, but she's working for G.C.E. and hasn't a lot of time.

PRIEST
Yes, but worse things happen at sea. Let's have a look at
things. What *did* the Doctor say?

COMMUNICANT
Well, he said it might be an ulcer. He asked me about all
these pains I've had and poked me around a bit. He gave me
a prescription for some tablets, told me to stick to milk and
grilled fish, and said he might have me X-rayed, but he didn't
say when, and he hasn't been for three days. Just left me
hanging. I'm getting browned off lying here, and I've eaten
so much fish I'm growing fins!

PRIEST
I think we've got to remember that doctors know what
they're doing. Relax, chum, and put yourself in his hands.

COMMUNICANT
I just can't do that: I've started wondering to-day whether
it might be cancer. That chap at work started like this—he
was dead in three months.

PRIEST
Well, *you're* not going to be dead in three months. Anyway,
there's nothing to be frightened of. . . .

COMMUNICANT

Yes, I know—I'm a pretty poor Christian.

PRIEST

I never said that. I should be an awful moaner if I were in your place. . . . Look, I'm not a doctor, I'm a priest, but I've got a shrewd suspicion that the doctor thinks it wouldn't do you any harm to rest a bit; he's going to try and treat your ulcer medically without operating—but you've just got to wait and see. A bit of rest *won't* do you any harm—you *have* been living it up a bit lately with all those long hours and you're not as young as you were.

COMMUNICANT

I suppose you're right, but it's a helluva bind. You won't see me at church on Sunday, anyway.

PRIEST

No . . . well . . . the Church has come to you. Although, I suppose you're the Church in this room.

COMMUNICANT

Yes, I've been looking through that Prayer Book. Do you know you're supposed to say "Peace be to this house" when you come in?

PRIEST

Yes, I said it silently as I was coming upstairs.

COMMUNICANT

We're not going to have that long service, are we?

PRIEST

No, it's a bit of a mouthful. I'll say one or two prayers and give you a blessing before I go—and I think I've stayed long enough already. But may I make just one suggestion—read Psalm 91 before you go to sleep to-night. It's the only thing that kept me going during the war. I'll come and see you in a day or two. We shall have to think about bringing you Communion sometime. We'll talk about that next time. Now, I'll give you a blessing——

(b) The "Not-so-fervent"

Woman of 52 with rheumatoid arthritis

PRIEST

Good morning, Mrs B. (*Takes her hand very carefully, sees her wince before he touches it*)

MRS B

Good morning, Reverend.

PRIEST

I'd better introduce . . .

MRS B

You will excuse the mess, won't you. My Italian woman's child is ill this morning, and she's sent a message round to say she can't come. She's very unreliable, but I must say she's good when she does come.

PRIEST

I'm the temporary Chaplain at the English Church. Somebody told me about you yesterday and I thought I'd come to see you.

MRS B

Well, that's very nice of someone. I'm not a very regular attender at church, I'm afraid. I used to go on Armistice Day with my husband, but since he died I don't think I've been at all.

PRIEST

How long have you lived here?

MRS B

We came out just before the War. My husband was in the Bank, then we were interned when the Germans came: he died in '48. I didn't have much money and I decided to stay on here. My daughter went home and got married there, then this arthritis started, and I've been more or less a prisoner ever since.

PRIEST

Do you ever get out at all?

MRS B

Oh yes, people are very kind and take me out occasionally. They bring me books from the English Library, and I've got my wireless set.

PRIEST

Do you have any treatment?

MRS B

Yes, I've had gold injections and all the rest. It's so expensive, though, and nothing seems to be really the answer.

PRIEST

And you have tablets to keep down the pain?

MRS B

Good heavens, yes. I take so many I'm sure I should rattle if you shook me. They make you feel so dopey, too.

PRIEST

Yes— I don't think I shall shake you!

MRS B

I don't know, but I don't feel that all that you stand for means much when you're like this.

PRIEST

You mean religion and all that?

MRS B

Yes—I feel very bitter at times, you know.

PRIEST

I'm sure *I* should, if I'd had all the disappointments you've had. But it doesn't get you very far. We just get more and more turned in on ourselves without much satisfaction for anybody.

MRS B

Yes, I know, but I have had a pretty poor life, haven't I? It doesn't seem quite fair, does it?

PRIEST

I think life's often very *un*fair.

MRS B

That's a funny thing for a parson to say.

PRIEST

Well, I ought to qualify it, I suppose. You see, I'm sure God is never unfair.

MRS B

I don't see it—I'm sorry.

PRIEST

Look, can I suggest something? You've got a Bible or a prayer book knocking about?

MRS B

I think there's a school Bible amongst some of my husband's books.

PRIEST

Just try and read in St Mark's Gospel about the unfairest thing that I think ever happened. If you want me to, I'll come round next week and we can talk about it. I ought to be going now—that sounds like your maid arriving. Good-bye and God bless you.

(c) The Complete Stranger

Man of 44 in later stages of carcinoma of the lung

PRIEST

Good afternoon, Mr. Smith.

MR SMITH

Afternoon. Who are you?

PRIEST

I'm the local Vicar. I've come to see Bill Jones in the next bed and he was talking about you. You're not so good, he tells me.

MR SMITH

Lousy. (Uses sputum cup)

PRIEST

How long have you been in?

MR SMITH

Seventeen weeks and I'm just about browned off.

PRIEST

It's a long time. You must have been in here at Christmas.

MR SMITH

Yes, looks as if I'll be here next Christmas as well.

PRIEST

Do you have a lot of pain?

MR SMITH

Yes, but they give me tablets to keep me happy. I don't think I'm getting any better. They tell me I am, but I'm losing weight all the time. I try to keep cheerful for the wife and kids—they come to see me twice a week—but I think I've had it.

PRIEST

What does the doctor say?

MR SMITH

Oh, they never tell you anything. Just got to have more tests or something.

PRIEST

Well, I don't suppose they can get to the bottom of things without tests. But I know it's a weary business. What's your job?

MR SMITH

Docker. But I don't think I shall go back to it. Things aren't what they were in the docks. I'd like a lighter job where you can earn money a bit easier.

PRIEST

It's a tough job; I've watched them unloading those Swedish boats from the Bridge.

MR SMITH

Yes, we always have a gallery. Ought to charge them entertainment tax.

PRIEST

It's always nice to watch other people working.

MR SMITH

Do you know, this is the first time I've ever spoken to a parson? I've only been to church twice in my life, once when I was christened and once last year when my girl was married.

PRIEST

Which church was that?

MR SMITH

It's . . . er . . . St James', I think. Vicar's an old chap, wouldn't allow photographs and kicked up a fuss about confetti. After all, it's only once in a lifetime. . . .

PRIEST

Yes, I know the church—and I know what a devil of a job it is getting confetti out of coconut matting!

MR SMITH

I can never tell what he's talking about. He's a bit like those chaps on the telly who are always getting at you for not going to church—I always switch it off.

PRIEST

I'm sorry we annoy you. We try to do our best.

MR SMITH

No, there's nothing personal. I don't mean you. But I don't like being preached at.

PRIEST

I don't think any of us do like it. All I want you to know is that the Church wants to help you in any way it can—and we shall be thinking about you to-night at Evensong for a start. I'll come and see you again, if you like—and would you like me to post that Pools coupon on your locker?

The reader will have perceived that these three interviews are all "open-ended" in that they are only the beginning of an exercise in pastoral ministry. The communicant with an ulcer is probably going to need surgery, the priest will follow him to hospital, and there will be seen the therapeutic effects of a "caring" community in convalescence and so on.

The lady exiled in a foreign land, who is an arthritic, may have to be led by a succession of chaplains and friends, who will form a therapeutic community, to a deeper understanding of the Christian religion and perhaps a reorientation of her existence in the care of some Christian agency.

Our docker friend may very well die without the consolation of sacraments, but he will have known the friendship and concern of a Christian minister, and will have realized that Christ's "strange work" comprehends more than not allowing confetti.

5

Following your Sick to Hospital

"There's an ambulance outside No. 16.
I believe Mr Jones is ill."

When Dr X has decided that Mr Jones needs more specialized treatment or is an emergency case, he telephones the
appropriate hospital, arranges his admission, sends off to the
hospital the necessary information on his case, and, for the
time being, the patient is out of his care and the G.P. may
not even see him until the time comes for his discharge and
he is returned to the care of the home practice.

This is not the case with pastoral care. Although each
hospital has either a full-time Church of England chaplain
(there are about ninety-six Church of England chaplains,
three Free Church, and two Roman Catholic in England and
Wales) or a part-time officiating chaplain, the pastoral supervision of the very large numbers of patients would be a quite
impossible task were the work of the officially appointed
chaplains not heavily supplemented by the visits of the
patients' own clergymen or ministers.

The official memorandum of the Ministry of Health on
this subject (H.M.C. (51) 31) states that a Management Committee or Board of Governors should appoint the chaplain,
or chaplains if there are more than one denomination, for
every hospital for which they are responsible, and these appointments should always be made in consultation with the
appropriate Church authorities. Most Regional Hospital
Boards have set up a Church of England Advisory Committee
which deals with the appointment of chaplains in the regions
concerned.

These appointments may be either whole-time or
part-time, and the Ministry leaves it to the Management

Committee or Board of Governors to decide whether a whole-time or part-time chaplain is required, and also which denominations should have a representative.

A guiding line has been suggested in so far as a whole-time appointment in any denomination should be considered only for units where the average number of patients in that denomination to be served is 750 or more, unless there are exceptional circumstances in which the Committee or Board feel justified in appointing a whole-time chaplain for a smaller unit. An obvious example of exceptional circumstances is seen in the case of a teaching hospital, where there may be only 500 Anglicans, and yet probably as many as 1,000 medical and dental students and 900 nurses.

The Ministry circular goes on to point out that *even where chaplains, whole-time or part-time, have been appointed, this does not detract from the right of any patient to be visited by his own parish priest or minister, if he so wishes.*

THE FUTURE

Various attempts have been made during recent years by responsible bodies to persuade the Ministry of Health that the number of 750 is too high and that whole-time chaplaincies ought to be established with greater liberality. It is not known whether the Ministry will see its way in the future to altering its "guiding line"; what is certain is that the "district hospital" of the future will be a much smaller and more comprehensive establishment than some of the enormous hospitals of the past. Whole-time chaplains may or may not be appointed, but the Church will in any case have to see to it that part-time chaplaincies are effectively filled and effectively exercised.

It is predictable, therefore, that the parish priest, so far from leaving his sick folk to the so-called specialized ministry of the hospital chaplain, will have to follow his people into hospital more assiduously than ever before if the work of the Church in the hospitals is to be carried on efficiently.

D

But what does efficiency in this sphere mean? Is it possible to calculate the effectiveness of the priest's ministry in terms of beddage and guiding lines? Is not our aim, too, to demonstrate that the Church is not only the priest, but the doctor, the nurse, the almoner, the hospital porter welding themselves into one therapeutic community?

Of course it is, and it is also part of the priest's task to teach men so, but the bed-to-bed, house-to-house, person-to-person ministry of the parson will ever remain the hard core of his pastoral mission.

There is said to be tragic division between the general practitioner, the "parish priest" of medicine, and the world of the consultant and registrar in hospitals. We must see that such a division never develops between parish priest and hospital chaplain.

THE HOSPITAL WORLD

It might be helpful for those who have never spent any length of time in hospital surroundings to know something about the organization of the National Health Service and the chains of command in the hospital world. Those who went into one of the services as chaplains during and after the war were grateful for the short courses of instruction which taught us how to tell the difference between a corporal and a colonel, how to salute the quarterdeck, how to indent for things, and how not to appear foolish and awkward on a battle-field.

Such courses for those who are to minister in hospitals have been organized for some years by the Hospital Chaplaincies Council of the Church Assembly, by the Church of England Hospital Chaplains' Fellowship, by various Diocesan Bishops, and by some Regional Hospital Boards. Best of all, pastoral clinical training courses of some six weeks' duration have been arranged at the Deva Hospital, Chester, and at St George's Hospital, Hyde Park Corner, by the Reverend Norman Autton. These courses include periods of

duty as a hospital porter and ward orderly, and enable ordinands or young priests to see from the inside the workings of
a large hospital. Any pastor who wishes to make his ministry
to the sick more effective would be well advised to take
advantage of these longer courses.

Amongst many other things, he will learn that for hospital
purposes our country is divided into nineteen regions. Each
region provides a complete hospital service with all of the
various specialist services. It is administered by a regional
hospital board and serves a population of an average of three
to four million people. Every large town has one or more
hospitals, which may be grouped together and are administered by hospital management committees, all of which are
responsible to the regional hospital board.

Each hospital is staffed by a team of consultant physicians
and surgeons (John Smith calls them "specialists") assisted
by teachers ("Registrars" who are real Doctors!) and house
physicians or surgeons, who are gaining experience with a
view to obtaining ultimately consultant posts, and others
who specialize in limited fields, such as anaesthetics, chest
diseases, mental diseases, and so on. The physicians and surgeons may be employed full-time or part-time. Those who
work part-time are entitled also to undertake private practice: they see patients at their own consulting rooms and
treat them in nursing homes and private wings of hospitals
where they charge fixed fees for their services.

Each hospital is staffed, in addition to doctors, by a com-
plement of nursing staff, which is under the direction of
a matron. These are employed by the hospital management committee, as is the staff responsible for administration, the engineers, the cooks, domestic staff, porters, and
so on.

The superintendent or hospital secretary, who need not
be a medical man, is like a managing director responsible
to his board of management. Sometimes he is called the
House Governor, sometimes the Secretary-Superintendent,
and sometimes the Medical Superintendent. It is a little

confusing, but it need puzzle us no more than the title of rural dean for someone who presides over an area in Manchester where there is only an occasional window-box to suggest the country.

From this apex of the triangle of command depend the various chains of command in the individual hospital, and we shall be wise to spend some time in mastering the pattern. The hospital world has its own traditions and etiquette, and the path of our ministry in this world will be made much smoother if we know the ropes and know how to avoid the pitfalls. It is not always possible to be a patient in hospital or to work in one as a porter or orderly or nurse: and so we shall try to follow—on paper—Mr Jones as he goes into hospital.

THE AMBULANCE OUTSIDE NO. 16

Mr Jones has been ill for some time with stomach trouble. The symptoms had indicated to the doctor that the colitis from which he was suffering might involve the necessity of surgery; he had called in specialist opinion, a consultant surgeon from the local hospital had paid a "domiciliary visit", and arrangements had been made for him to "have a bed" as soon as one was available. Mr Jones had wondered ruefully why things could not move a little more quickly. He had had to wait a few days for the consultant to come. The specialist had been very charming, had asked him lots of questions, his strong, clean fingers had kneaded his stomach, he had looked wise and thoughtful, had exchanged cryptic remarks with long words in them with the G.P., and had finally shaken hands with "Well, Mr Jones, I think we'd better have you into hospital for a day or two; we can do some tests there better than we can here. We'll soon have your tummy better. Don't worry—I'll go back to the hospital now and see if there's a bed available."

Mr Jones had thought that things were really moving quickly now and that he would be in hospital within twenty-four hours at least. But he had not realized (how could he have?) that all that consultant's eighteen beds were occupied, and that no patient was due to be discharged for a week. There were two more urgent cases on the consultant's waiting list, and unless Mr Jones was classed as "an emergency", it was unlikely that he would be admitted to hospital for at least three weeks.

There had been telephone calls to the hospital and visits from the patient's own doctor, and Mr Jones had been assured that he had not been forgotten and that "as soon as there was a bed" he would get a card from the hospital.

After a fortnight's waiting and acute discomfort (his colitis had not improved) he became very angry and gave himself up to bitter complaints about the National Health Service, hospitals, specialists "driving about in their posh Rolls-Royces", his wife, his family ("they weren't a bit sympathetic"), and life in general. The Vicar came in for some of this, as it was about this time that he first called.

At the end of nearly three weeks the card did drop through the letter-box one morning, and the following day an ambulance arrived. There was great excitement in the street: some people came out of their doors and shouted encouragingly, others looked round their curtains shyly and heads were nodded in rhythmic sympathy.

The ambulance men were very friendly and helped Mr Jones from his bed to the stretcher with great gentleness. They wrapped him in more blankets than he thought necessary, negotiated the narrow staircase with great skill ("I suppose you have a lot of this to do.") and carried him out into the fresh air which seemed to hit him like something new. He suddenly realized that he had never been outside his house for seven weeks.

The men slipped the stretcher into its slots in the ambulance; Mrs Jones climbed in with a hold-all. "I've got your shaving things, a tooth-brush, a spare pair of pyjamas, your pen and some writing paper: I'll get you some nice soap and bring it to-morrow." One of the ambulance men goes to the front and starts the engine, the other stays to make Mrs Jones comfortable.

As they move smoothly off, the patient notices that it is difficult to see out of the windows and tries to recognize the route to the hospital by the outlines of the buildings and the turns in the various streets. He talks to his wife, "You know, I'm not going for weeks, all this talk about spare night clothes and things. I shall be back in a day or two." He discovers from the ambulance man that they are not from the hospital but from a sort of pool. "Dial 999 and all that?" Mr Jones feels vaguely excited but deeply anxious inside.

He feels the ambulance turn in slowly and then reverse. The doors are flung open. Ambulance men and porters confer, a smart-looking nurse appears with some papers in her hand, smiles at Mr Jones and says reassuringly, "We'll soon have you fixed up. Take him to 'Admission'." The patient is wheeled down a corridor into an atmosphere of purposeful bustle, into the hospital smell compounded of floor polish, disinfectant, cooking odours, and the dispensing department of the local chemist's.

Then the waiting. A famous consultant once said to us that "all waiting in hospital is not evil, you know", and it is doubtless true that great grace comes to souls who wait patiently, but Mr Jones may perhaps be forgiven for thinking that he has been forgotten as the minutes tick by, and all he can see is the bare walls of the examination room and his wife smiling at him suddenly when he catches her eye.

"If they keep me waiting much longer I shall disgrace myself." The colitis is making its presence urgently felt when a young lady in a crisp white coat with a tight, blue belt comes in with what looks like an adding machine. It is a device for making several carbon copies of the admission slip which she proceeds to write out. "May I have some details, Mr Jones?" Name, address, name of local doctor, telephone number or nearest police station, next of kin, religious denomination, what sort of admission, emergency or waiting list or from casualty, age, occupation.

Our patient wonders why all this is needed. He had only come for a few tests for a day or two. "Well, you see, one copy goes to the ward, one to records, one to the chaplain, one to the Matron's Office." He decides it is all part of the red tape which he has heard about; he will learn later how necessary such documentation really is, but he cannot be expected to comprehend its purpose as he lies there without any of the familiar landmarks of his daily life—his job, his home, his garden, his television set, his little car, the "Esq." on his letters—to fortify him.

"This patient to C 14 Surgical Block. I've rung the ward and they're getting a bed ready." An older-looking Staff Nurse (more impressive looking badges and a dark belt) gives the order to two porters in brown coats, and they wheel Mr Jones away down two long corridors, into a lift which takes them very gently (although, Mr Jones notices, it does rock a bit) to the third floor, down two more corridors, and through two swing doors which nearly knock down Mrs Jones who is still keeping up the rear.

"Ah, Mr Jones: I think we're almost ready for you. We'll soon have you in bed. Is this Mrs Jones? Perhaps you'd like to sit in my office until we get your husband settled. There are some magazines there. Perhaps you'd like a cup of tea. Eleanor, make Mrs Jones a pot of tea—she can have it in my office." Eleanor, the ward maid, who is wearing a plain over-all, goes off to the kitchen and for the twentieth time that day makes a pot of tea.

Before the Sister (dark dress with a rather more elaborate hat than the others) goes into the ward to supervise the trans-lation of Mr Jones from the trolley to the bed, Mrs Jones says, "Excuse me, Sister" and whispers in her ear. "Now don't worry—we'll see to that. Nurse, see that Mr Jones is com-fortable: I think he needs some attention urgently."

Our patient now feels that things are really moving. Capable hands are making him feel that he is secure; although he feels very high up in the world in his hospital bed and that perhaps they might not have made his bed so tightly that it feels like an envelope, he is conscious of security for the first time since his illness began.

A young student nurse (no belt, plain cap) comes to Mr Jones's bed with something under a cloth, draws the curtains round the bed, and says without any embarrassment, "I think you want one of these. I don't suppose you've used one. It's quite simple, really, and don't worry—we don't mind one little bit."

What many people think will be the ultimate embarrassment in hospital is "got over with" very early in Mr Jones's hospital experience. When the curtains are drawn back and he looks round at the other twenty-four beds and sees smiles and knowing nods from other men's faces, his feelings are rather like those of the boy who has survived his first night at boarding school.

When his wife comes in and tries to arrange things a little more tidily on his locker, the feeling of embarrassment returns as he notices the other men looking down the ward, and he wishes with all his heart that she would go; the atmosphere is that of a railway station when one has said good-bye to a departing passenger and the train seems never to go.

"He'll be all right, Missus. We'll look after him, won't we, George?" Mrs Jones and her husband kiss one another, feeling as if a spotlight is turned on them, and the wife hurries out of the ward, meets the Sister at the door. "He will be all right, won't he, Sister? When can I come and see him?" Mrs Jones is told what the visiting hours are, when and where to ring up, and—"Don't worry."

AND NOW—MORE WAITING

Our patient becomes the observer of hospital life. The regular round of meals, temperature taking, bed-making, visiting hours, visits to X-ray, physiotherapy, Matron's round, the consultants' ward rounds, the predatory activities of the "leeches" from the Haematology Department who come for blood samples, the almoner's visits. . . . Mr Jones realizes slowly that a hospital is a place of intense activity where the "day or two for tests" which the specialist had promised for him have to be geared into an extensive programme of medical and surgical work constructed round hundreds and thousands of cases like his own.

Theologians tell us that we have got the wrong conception of "time": it is certainly true that the medical profession on the whole have a different conception of time from that of Mr Jones. And it is during the waiting that we shall often have to visit Mr Jones as pastors.

6

The Priest Visits in Hospital

"How long are you going to keep me here?"

The National Health Service Act of 1946 lays upon the Minister of Health the duty "to promote the establishment in England and Wales of a comprehensive health service designed to secure improvement in the physical and mental health of the people of England and Wales and the prevention, diagnosis and treatment of illness and for that purpose to provide or secure the effective provision of services in accordance with the following conditions of this Act".

One of these services would appear to consist in "providing for the spiritual needs of both patients and staff, and in particular to do everything possible so to arrange the hours of duty of nurses and other staff (and students at teaching hospitals) as to enable them to attend the services of their own denomination" (H.M.C. 51 (31)).

It would seem, therefore, that the priest need have no fear that he will have no place in a hospital or that his help or presence will be unwanted or unrecognized.

Now it has been said that whereas our tradition of nursing care in this country stems from Christian sources in the sickrooms of monastic establishments in the Middle Ages, our medical science has its roots in pre-Christian ages, and therefore the secularist might suggest that the Christian minister is intruding into fields not his own when he visits in hospital. Our answer would be that we believe that all healing work is of God, and wherever it is going on, there we ought to be as his ministers.

Although we are protected, as it were, by statute and our ministry is approved by long tradition, we shall be most unwise to harbour any presumptions about the place which a priest has, or ought to have, in the hospital world. We cannot take for granted such privileges as the Church enjoys in the hospital field, and it is perfectly possible for the National Health Service Act to be interpreted by a local Regional Hospital Board in such a way that the work of the Church is made very difficult.

It behoves us, therefore, to see that we take every opportunity of using our privileges *efficiently and courteously*. From our knowledge of the Regional Boards in this country and most of the teaching hospitals we would say without hesitation that there is an abundance of goodwill towards the visiting clergyman. But we are familiar with most, if not all, of the complaints about him!

WE GO TO SEE MR JONES

If he is not dangerously ill and this is what one might term a routine visit, we shall be careful to choose an hour which is not likely to be inconvenient to the staff. If we go to the Porter's Lodge or the Inquiry Office, we shall treat the clerk or the porter with the same respect as we should accord to the Consultant. We need not go nervously about our task, but "I wonder if it would be possible for me to visit Mr Jones in C7?" can be said with just as much effectiveness and considerably more courtesy than "Mr Jones—which ward's he in?"

We find our way to the ward and are careful to wait until we are given permission to enter. "Oh, I always breeze straight in, they don't mind" may be the remark of a priest who always causes the nursing staff to go and fume in the privacy of the ward kitchen. We shall remember that the Ward Sister (or in her absence, the Staff Nurse or senior nurse on duty) is the hostess of the ward and we are her guests.

There are some occasions when the ward is "closed"— when the doors are closed and there are screens round the beds. It may be bed-making or bed-pan rounds, and it is obviously inconvenient for us to go into the ward. We should not show our impatience and tell our long story of funerals and meetings which have filled our day. The nurses have been very busy, too.

When we have become accepted by the nursing staff and have won their confidence, it is highly likely that we may be asked to wait a minute or two, a nurse will be sent off to "tidy-up" Mr Jones, and we shall be allowed to creep round the screens for a few minutes with him. But don't presume!

There are other times when "there's a doctor in the ward" who may be a Consultant with his team or "firm" of Registrar and House Surgeons or Physicians. The latter two are recently qualified doctors who are in charge of patients, but who do not have the ultimate responsibility for them. The team is completed by a handful of medical students.

A Consultant's round is a dignified occasion when it is customary to have strict silence in the ward and the Ward Sister is in attendance (with her cuffs on) with the specialist. Generally it is unwise to ask for permission to go into the ward at these times. If you ask a junior nurse, she has to tip-toe down the ward to ask the Sister, the Sister may say No, and the nurse has to return, running the gauntlet of twenty-odd pairs of men's eyes, watching her with sympathetic amusement, and then she has to say, blushingly, "Sister says No".

A Registrar's round is less formal; he may be teaching round somebody's bed or in a corner of the ward. It is possible that the Ward Sister will give you permission to go into the ward, but remember the occasions you have tried to preach in a church with the windows open and there has been a "ton-up boy" revving his motor-cycle outside. Registrars like sympathy, too. Don't talk too loudly.

The H.P.'s or H.S.'s round takes place once or twice every day. The young doctor is very conscious of his position and his responsibilities. It is a courteous act to ask if you may see Mr Jones whilst he is doing his round. The Sister may ask you into her office for a cup of tea afterwards. The

Houseman will probably be there. Both of you will come to the conclusion afterwards that you really do belong to the same species.

ASKING QUESTIONS

Your natural curiosity will make you want to know what is wrong with Mr Jones, how long he is going to be in, when they are going to operate, and so on. It would be nice to be in the know when one of Mr Jones's neighbours meets you in the street to-morrow. It is best to confine one's initial inquiries to "How is Mr Jones to-day, Sister?" If one persists with "Do you think he's going to need surgery?" or be-spatters one's conversation with technical terms, the staff will assume that one is merely being at pains to demonstrate a knowledge of medical dictionaries and they will become reticent and retire into an amused silence.

This is not to say that once confidence has been established between the priest and the nursing staff there will not be the utmost frankness and a sometimes embarrassing wealth of clinical detail poured into the ears of the discreet pastor, but we have to wait for that.

Further, it should always be remembered that a junior nurse is instructed never to divulge any details of patients' illnesses to anybody save her superiors, and we put Junior Nurse X into a very awkward position if we insist on storming her integrity with a barrage of questions.

The priest is not permitted to read the patient's chart or case papers. These are confidential and should not be read even by the patient himself, although we all know the "wide boys" who have crawled down the bed when nobody is looking to "have a dekko" at the chart. The latest trick, now that mobile bedside telephones are coming more and more into use, is to ring up the hospital to find out how you are! (The writer used to look at the local evening newspaper to see whether he'd been taken off the danger list—in those days, we all had a number, and bulletins were published in the press every day.)

But really, it may be impatiently asked, how are we going to perform our task intelligently and co-operate with the medical and nursing staff if we are to be content to be left in the dark like this? The answer is that we shall not be left in the dark if we demonstrate, by our courtesy and willingness to accept the discipline of hospital etiquette, that we are anxious to help the patient and ready to co-operate with doctor and nurse alike. Then we shall be treated as allies; mutual respect and confidence will grow, and we shall feel that we really are part of the "healing team".

It is possible to gather enough information from one's conversation with Mr Jones, without any sort of probing, to be able to assess the medical situation.

LET US GO ALONG TO BED 22

There are other people in the ward besides Mr Jones. Sometimes they are sleeping, sometimes unconscious (just come back from the theatre, there is a drip working, and a nurse is adjusting a kidney bowl)—some reading newspapers—some listening to the wireless through "pillophones"—all interested in this new figure coming into their little community. Ever since they woke up this morning there has been a never-ending procession of visitors—porters, newsboys, barbers, night superintendent, doctors, assistant matrons, haematologist, radiologists, almoners, food trolleys, porters with the letters—you may be the first parson to-day. They are all interested and study your progress down the ward. Whether we like it or not and whether it is justified or not, there will be a very critical assessment of our demeanour. It is Mr Jones we have come to see, but surely we can spare a smile, a nod, or a "Good afternoon" as we pass the other beds.

We arrive at Bed No. 22. Mr Jones blushes slightly because he seems to be the one picked out for a visit. The nurse brings us a chair. "Would you like the curtains drawn, sir?" We politely decline and may shake hands with the patient if he extends his hand—but no prolonged or hearty handshakes!

MR JONES

Well, it's nice of you to come, Vicar.

PRIEST

I wanted to see how you are getting on. How are you feeling to-day?

MR JONES

Oh, fairly comfortable but my old tummy is playing me up. I had an awful night last night. I couldn't sleep there was so much noise in the ward. That chap's very ill over there and they had to have the doctor up twice in the night. They can't help making a bit of disturbance—they're very kind, though, and by jingo, those young nurses work hard.

PRIEST

Which doctor have you seen?

MR JONES

Well, there are two—an oldish one who came to see me yesterday. He examined me and looked at my chart but he didn't say much. The other one's a Pakistani but he's very nice, talked to me a lot about Karachi—I was there during the war—he says I've got to have some tests. They wouldn't let me have any breakfast this morning—I had to eat a lot of white stuff—it was awful—then they took me down for an X-ray.

PRIEST

Yes, Barium meal, I think they call it.

MR JONES

What I'd like to know is—and I asked him to-day—"How long are you going to keep me here?" He just laughed and said, "We'll get you right first".

PRIEST

Well, that's it, isn't it? There's no point in coming in unless you're going to be put right.

MR JONES

Yes, but Vicar—what about my job? And the family?

PRIEST

Now they are all right. I went to see your wife this morning.

She's been to see them at work and they've sent your wages—
I think your wife is going to see the Almoner to-morrow
about some of the H.P. payments. Most firms are insured
against cases like this and you'll be all right—there's nothing
for you to worry about at all.

MR JONES

But Dr X said it would only be for a day or two. And most of
the people in here seem to be having operations. Do you
think they're going to operate on me?

PRIEST

I don't know. I suppose they are making all these tests to
find out what would be the best thing to do. And, after all, if
it has to be an operation, there's nothing to be frightened of
—they are first-class people here—and thousands of other
people have had them—I've had one or two myself. You're a
bit frightened at the time, but I'm very glad I had them now.

MR JONES

It's a bit different at my age. I've got a family depending on
me. I've been wondering what I've done to deserve all this.

PRIEST

I shouldn't worry about that! We don't always get ill as a
punishment for what we've done wrong. Otherwise some of
us would spend our whole lives in hospital. When you say
your prayers to-night ask God to forgive you anything you've
done wrong in the past—we always ought to do that.

MR JONES

It's a long time since I said any prayers.

PRIEST

Well, it's a good time to start when you're in hospital. You
know the Lord's Prayer—well, say it slowly to-night—thinking about what each bit means. I used to spend nearly all day
on it when I was in hospital once.

MR JONES

The chaplain came round yesterday asking if anybody
wanted Holy Communion—but I've never been confirmed.

I was supposed to be but something went wrong and I've never got round to it.

PRIEST

We shall have to see about that when you're out. It's a very normal thing for older men to be prepared for confirmation.

MR JONES

The wife has been—and the daughters.

PRIEST

I presented someone at the age of 87 for confirmation the other day.

MR JONES

I don't think I shall live that long somehow.

PRIEST

You've as much chance as anybody. I'm going now—I promised Sister I wouldn't be too long. I think you may just be able to hear our church bell from here. When you hear it to-morrow morning, remember we shall be thinking about you at the Eucharist. I'll come and see you again. Good-bye, and God bless you.

With people who are much more seriously ill than Mr Jones, conversations like this are not practicable. Our visits should be much shorter, and it is often a good thing to have the curtains drawn if they are not already round the bed. We have probably been told by the Sister that the patient is rather poorly and cannot talk much. We should adopt a much more gentle approach, taking the patient's hand carefully and introducing ourselves quietly.

Suggestions about the kind of prayers and blessings to be used will be found in manuals referred to in the Bibliography at the end of this volume.

Our purpose now must be to evaluate the question uppermost in Mr Jones's mind, "How long are they going to keep him there?"

E

7

Assessing the Situation

"There are no atheists in hospital."

We leave the ward and we leave Mr Jones to the good-natured banter of his fellow-patients. We have said "thank-you" to the Sister or Staff Nurse; if the ward is not busy, we may have been invited into the Sister's office for a cup of tea drunk out of her best china. If we are wise we shall never spurn such invitations as it is during such occasions that we shall learn a great deal about hospital methods and about our own patients.

We shall not forget to do the courteous thing and leave our card or a note in the Chaplain's pigeon-hole at the Porter's Lodge to acquaint him of the fact that we have been in "his" hospital and to commend to his pastoral care Mr Jones, explaining the number of his ward, whether he is a communicant, and so on.

It may be that we are already on friendly terms with the doctor in charge of his case and can without formality leave him a note, too, saying that Mr Jones is one of the people in whom we have an interest.

As we proceed to our next appointment we shall be assessing the situation. Our patient is in a "surgical" ward; we know that this probably indicates that an operation is a possibility. We have discovered that one can be just as ill in a "medical" ward but that a "physician" looks after you there and tries to treat you without having recourse to the operating theatre.

From other cases we have known and from our conversations with medical friends we know with a certain rough precision that the "tests" will consist of giving Mr Jones a barium enema (which he had been too shy to mention) and barium meals, followed by X-rays (the gut filled with barium is opaque to X-ray) and the use of a screen to enable the surgeon to see if there was any abnormal movement in Mr Jones's colon. The consultant and registrar would talk a great deal about differential diagnosis, and whether the facts they had elicited from the plates established the presence of carcinoma, or whether it was ulcerative colitis which could be treated medically. If there had to be surgery it would be either a colectomy or a colostomy; if it could be dealt with by the physicians it would be by means of diet and drugs such as chloromycetin.

Our very amateur analysis of the situation would not mean that we should go round to the family and blind them with science (we might be wrong, anyway), but it would mean that we should have a fairly clear idea of what might be possible on a spiritual plane.

If there is going to be an operation, we ought to go to Mr Jones on the night before he "goes down to the theatre" and without dramatizing the situation reassure him, giving him a blessing and promising him the support of our congregation's prayers the following morning. It might be that Mr Jones might want to say something to the priest—perhaps an informal confession of something that has been on his conscience for a long time, perhaps a purely practical matter of where his will is to be found if anything happens . . . "It won't, but just in case."

We also know that ulcerative colitis can also be induced by anxiety or some unhappiness. We may not know of anything, and he may be unconscious of it himself, but it is often the case that a person will confide in the parson things which he would not dream of telling anybody else. We shall always avoid ever thinking of ourselves as amateur psychiatrists or as being in some kind of way superior to that science, but we shall never underrate in any way our rôle as shepherd of souls.

Further, we know roughly that it takes a week or more to complete such tests as these which Mr Jones is undergoing before the decision is taken by his doctors. We have time to plan our moves—another visit in three days' time? Sending his name to the community of nuns who pray for our sick folk? Wonder if he would like one of those little prayer cards?

ESTABLISHING LIAISON WITH THE HEALING COMMUNITY

After our next visit to hospital things will be a little clearer. The Ward Sister and the nurses are beginning to know who we are: sometimes it is helpful to leave one's address and telephone number. We shall have found out by looking in the hospital chapel or talking on the telephone to the hospital chaplain what religious ministrations are available in the hospital. It may be that ward services are held regularly, it may be a relay from the hospital chapel that comes over the piped radio, perhaps Mr Jones might like to know what religious services are available on the B.B.C.

Whatever the arrangements, it can safely be said that a commendation of a hospital patient to the official chaplain by a parish priest is more important than anything else. The failure of so many parish priests to commend their people is quite lamentable. Even where there is a whole-time chaplain at work it is quite impracticable for him to make contact immediately with every one of the patients who are admitted to the hospital. Although he may have daily lists of admissions sent to his office, it is often not possible for him to see each patient within even forty-eight hours of his entry into the hospital world, especially in a large hospital where there may be anything up to two hundred and fifty admissions each week. But if a commendation from a parish priest comes in, the chaplain will be at pains to go immediately to the patient concerned. We have known cases where the parochial clergyman has complained bitterly about the neglect of his people by the hospital chaplain without ever having intimated to him by letter or telephone the presence in the wards of his churchwarden or some daily communicant. Sometimes it would almost appear that the parish priests have become so possessive about "their" people that they resent any pastoral supervision by anybody else, and just wait for the hospital chaplain to make a mistake. The young priest should always remember that the full-time hospital chaplain is performing a task which is well-nigh impossible, is probably working twelve hours a day, and with the turn-over in patients increasing annually feels more and more like a hen, in Keble Talbot's memorable phrase, "trying to lay an egg on an escalator". So we shall never despise commendations.

OTHER HEALING AGENCIES

Mr Jones has come into hospital to be made whole. He will have expert medical and nursing care. Experienced eyes and minds will watch and assess his case history, the results of tests, his temperature charts, his reaction, both physical and mental, to life in a hospital ward or private room. Pastoral care will be exercised not only by the priest but by those who visit him during visiting hours, by those who bring round the library trolley, by the almoner's staff who will help him with any concern about national insurance or hire-purchase payments, but also by the other patients in the same ward who exercise a kind of "group therapy" with their attitudes to sickness and pain. A real kind of community spirit is engendered in a well-run ward.

Mr Jones will be reassured by the fact that Mr Smith in the next bed is recovering very successfully from *his* operation and is due to be discharged in a few days' time. He becomes interested in the progress of Mr Brown at the end of the ward who has been badly injured in a bus crash, and he becomes fascinated by the variety of delicacies which his wife brings each evening, ranging from stewed eels to black puddings. He listens with patience and wonderment to the saga of Mr X's matrimonial involvements. Mr Jones's mental horizons become very much widened. He realizes that his own troubles are not the only ones in the world.

And—most importantly for him—he begins to feel the real concern that his fellow-patients feel for him. They are anxious to help him to feel at home, to learn the ropes, to master the ward rules and the hospital time-table; they explain the difference between a student nurse and a staff nurse, and how to get hold of the electric razor. He learns that they are really rather pleased when they see Mr Jones's Vicar come into the ward, and pass complimentary remarks when he seems "human" and speaks to them quite naturally.

Mr Jones will always remember the remark of a fellow-patient: "You know, you see a lot of awful things happening in hospital (I shall never forget a child of two dying of cancer), but you see so many wonderful things happening and people are so kind that you just can't be an atheist in hospital."

THEY DECIDE ON SURGERY

At the end of ten days the Consultant comes to see Mr Jones and tells him that they have decided that the best thing in the long run would be to do a little operation. There would be nothing to worry about, it would be a simple operation that would put him right for good, and his tummy troubles would be at an end. For the sake of his wife and family he ought to have it done. The Consultant knew hundreds of men who had had this operation and were now back at work leading useful and happy lives. If Mr Jones gave his permission, the operation could be done next Thursday—perhaps he would think about it and talk to his wife when she came that evening.

When the doctor has gone, Mr Jones lies in silence for a few minutes, his muscles tensed, and feels rather like a parachutist recruit sitting on the edge of the hole in the captive balloon, whose instincts scream at him to draw back but who is unwilling to face the scornful looks of his officers and fellow-recruits if he does. "Are you going down, then?" from the next bed breaks the silence, and Mr Jones nods assent.

The next few days of waiting will be tense and anxious days for Mr Jones, whether the operation be of a major or minor character. Indeed, Russell Dicks has wisely said that from the patient's point of view there is no such thing as a "minor operation". Most people are apprehensive when they face surgery, although they may be more familiar with operating theatre scenes than they were a generation ago. The tense and dramatic moments in surgery which have been presented to us on television screens in recent years may have made us more knowledgeable, but it is doubtful whether they have made us less fearful when we are personally involved.

So we shall try to be quietly reassuring with Mr Jones during the period of waiting. We shall pray for the surgeon as well as for Mr Jones. Into thy hands we commend the body and soul of Bill Jones—into God's hands and into the surgeon's hands as he performs God's healing work the surgeon's hands wield the knife but it is God's hands that heal. . . .

We shall be careful not to dramatize the situation, but may suggest for our patient's reading Psalm 139 or passages such as Matthew 6.30–4. We may say with Mr Jones, or give him a card with this prayer:

> Jesu, Friend and Brother,
> Who didst suffer upon the Cross
>   For love of me;
> Help me to feel thee near me.
> Hold my hand in thy strong, pierced hand,
> That I may be brave and patient
>   For love of thee.

In some cases it is possible to take Holy Communion to a patient on the morning of the operation. We should be quite sure that the pre-medication is not going to be given at an hour which will interfere with this. It may be preferable to take the Sacrament on the day before or even in the late evening. If our patient has been a regular communicant, he will welcome this and the priest will have little hesitation in suggesting it. If our patient is a lapsed communicant, the priest will take a great deal of care in his preparing of the ground before he suggests it, otherwise the patient's apprehensiveness may be increased rather than lessened.

WE MINISTER
TO THE FAMILY, TOO

The feelings of tension and apprehensiveness are not confined to the patient. His whole family is involved in this operation, and they will need our help and support almost as much as the patient. Sometimes it is possible for the family to come to church on the morning of the operation to pray for "Pop": in any case they will be glad to know that the Church is interceding for its sick member at its services. In other cases, a shy and lonely wife will welcome the priest's support as she waits in the hospital waiting room. There are sympathy and cups of tea in abundance in a hospital, but often a waiting relative outside a ward can be the loneliest of creatures—and it is a loneliness which can be assuaged by no set prayers or neat formula; it can be met only with compassionate sympathy and care.

THE OPERATION
WAS SUCCESSFUL . . .

. . . and Mr Jones has had a comfortable night. Our initial visits to Mr Jones after the operation will not be lengthy. We shall share in his joy and relief that it is all over and assure him of our confidence that he is going to make a complete recovery, of the rejoicing amongst his friends, and the thanksgivings that are being offered at the altar of his parish church.

DEDICATED PEOPLE

At the heart of this episode in Mr Jones's life—and it may rightly be described as a very "formative" episode—lies the period of time during which he was quite unconscious of what was going on around him, when he was on the operating table in the surgeon's hands.

In the theatre the concentrated attention of a whole team of surgeons, anaesthetists, sister, nurses, and technicians is directed towards a small area of Mr Jones's anatomy, and their efforts are concerned with his eternal destiny however unacquainted they may be with his character, his spiritual health, his family and social relationships, and so on. They are striving for his "wholeness" in regard to one disorder or malfunctioning of the body-mind-spirit nexus which is Mr Jones.

Those who have done any work in television studios will know how closely the atmosphere of rehearsal and performance of a TV programme resembles that of an operating theatre, and how easily the word "dedicated" slips into one's thinking as one sees the agonizing striving for perfection on the part of sound engineers, lighting experts, and vision mixers. The performers in an operating theatre are no less perfectionist and "dedicated". Their aim and object is a perfectly completed surgical operation.

The task of the pastor is to deal with the whole man—the total Mr Jones. May we be as dedicated as the team in the operating theatre who are dealing with a few inches of gut inside him! There may be exaggeration in the words of the patient who said there were no atheists in a hospital ward, but one cannot exaggerate the selfless devotion and dedication to be found amongst many of those who practise the healing arts in hospitals.

8

Special Cases

"He's so adaptable."

Just as every parish in the world has its own especial problems and is different from every other parish, so are sick people unique in their individual attitudes and circumstances. But when we speak of "special cases" we are referring to broad classes which are distinguishable from the Mrs Smith and Mr Jones whom we have been considering.

The secret of all effective pastoral work is for the priest to be adaptable. The single-minded young priest fights shy of this quality sometimes because it has the connotation of being "all things to all men" and being neither hot nor cold. "Mr Facing-both-ways" and the Vicar of Bray leap into his imagination as warning figures. Dealing with the special cases which are going to be discussed in this chapter will involve us in the shedding of many of the ingrained fundamentalisms, whether of the biblical or ecclesiastical varieties, which inhibit our pastoral ministry.

BLIND PEOPLE

The first thing to remember is that people without sight are possessed of an experience which has never been ours. They may have missed many of the fulfilments and delights which have come our way, but their perceptions have been sharpened in divers manners in a kind of compensation. Verbal images become more important. Our speaking to them must be slower and more deliberate. Manual acts become even more important—the handshake, the blessing, the gentle approach. The colour of the stole becomes much less important than the fact of it!

Those who can read braille can enjoy the comfort of the Scriptures, but if they are too ill to do this the reading by the minister of passages of the Bible will be of great help. Even the parish magazine can be of absorbing interest and spiritual help to some of our communicants.

We remember one blind patient who became terribly deaf as well. Our administration of Holy Communion to her became a ministry of touch. We began the Our Father together, our hands holding hers, we said the general confession together (her hands folded), she received absolution (the priest tracing a cross on her forehead), she received the wafer after the priest had touched her lips and the Blessing with the priest's hands laid on her head.

THE DEAF AND DUMB

Here visual images *are* important. The smile on the face of the priest, his expressions, his composed demeanour are always important, but in cases where the patient is dependent on his sight alone, of supreme importance. It is helpful for the pastor to learn a few of the words and phrases used in the sign language which is the *lingua franca* of the world of the hard of hearing. Very often the patient is able to lip-read, and if we remember to speak very slowly and deliberately, exaggerating slightly the movement of our lips, we shall be able to converse and say what we have to say—which may be less than we might say to somebody with perfect hearing, but ought to be no less reassuring and helpful for all its conciseness!

We ought always to call on the services of the experienced Missioner to the Deaf and Dumb, who works in each diocese or district, when difficulties arise or when the occasion demands less amateur efforts than our own. There are two things which might be added: If we are to preach to deaf and dumb congregations with the aid of an interpreter, we must be prepared to have gusts of laughter two sentences after we have made our favourite joke; otherwise we may be led to think that our "listeners" have missed the point. The other thing is that our physical movements, at the altar, for instance, can be used to underline the meaning of what we are doing and our message. The dramatic quality of a service has to be picked out visually.

MATERNITY CASES

"And is this your youngest?" was the remark of the young deacon at the bed-side of a mother in a maternity hospital. He felt ill at ease: he was in a very unfamiliar world: a world where small babies lay in cots with strips of sticking plaster on their wrists bearing names and dates: a world where slightly embarrassed ladies in flowered house coats moved with difficulty, and a door marked in forbidding black paint "Labour Ward" swung to and fro on his right hand. Two of the expectant mothers in the first half of the ward had giggled as he came in, and a large Irish Staff Nurse had been studiedly rude to him.

Except in cases of emergency it is not usually necessary for a priest to visit in a maternity ward except during recognized hours and other times when arrangements have been made with the Ward Sister. The minister will be wise to make himself familiar with ward routine and practice.

If the new-born baby and mother are doing well, we share in the joy of the parents and offer our congratulations and good wishes. Some thankful mothers will wish to receive Holy Communion in thanksgiving, especially if a Sunday is near: sometimes the priest may be asked to say a short thanksgiving at the bed-side. It is possible for this to be done quite simply without any fuss.

Great care must be exercised when the child has been still-born or is premature or deformed. We have to deal with someone who is bitterly disappointed, and we shall not be shocked or outraged when we hear God blamed or our ministry spurned. It is at moments like these when deeply dejected parents need most surely their pastor's loving care and understanding. Often both parents are troubled with strong feelings of guilt because they feel that it is because of "something they have done".

We shall find it helpful to have a private talk with the Ward Sister or the Midwife or the Doctor about Mrs X before we see her. We shall be able to reassure her that it is not because of some defect in her life or character that the baby has been born dead or deformed. We shall be careful not to say the dangerously easy "Never mind, you can always have another".

Superstitions abound in matters connected with childbirth, and while we should not go round a ward pouring scorn, right, left, and centre, on all desires to be "churched" and all protestations that "it will never thrive until it's been taken to church and 'done' ", we shall be at pains to instruct our people patiently about thanksgiving after childbirth and about Holy Baptism. One of the things we can take in our hands as we go into the maternity ward is the attractively illustrated book on Baptism which many hospital chaplains now distribute to their maternity patients.

The priest should be prudent when dealing with unmarried mothers. They are often known in a maternity ward as "Mrs So-and-so", and cheap wedding rings are easily available for their stay. He should be careful not to be dogmatic in his advice as to whether the mother should keep her child or not. There are many considerations to be taken into account, and the advice of a Moral Welfare Worker should be sought.

There are the cases where Mongol or hydrocephalic children are born to parents, who will ask for our advice as to whether they should let the child go into an institution for the care of such infants or whether they should keep it themselves. This is the point where we should counsel prolonged thought by everybody concerned and the expert advice of doctor and welfare officer before we presume to give advice. Perhaps we shall help most by assisting the parents to understand what either course of action would involve and by quoting "for and against" examples in our own experience. So much, too, depends on the spiritual maturity of the people concerned.

A young couple of our acquaintance have brought up with great devotion a child of their marriage who is both physically and mentally retarded. Throughout the child's life they have had to take it in turns to sit up at nights, and they have never been able to take a holiday together. They do not regard themselves as being in any way heroic; they have merely felt that it was their duty to care for the offspring they had brought into the world. We have known other cases where the child has been put in the care of the County authority when the parents, though relieved of the incessant demands of caring for it day after day, have been able to visit it regularly. (The situation is, of course, different when there are other children in the family.)

It need hardly be said that the priest should deal with all such cases with the greatest of tact. Parents do not like it to be known that they have an imbecile or deformed child. Old wives' tales about such cases being due to sexual incapacity on the part of one or other of the parents and ill-digested teaching about "the sins of the fathers" are always being quoted by unthinking relatives. We have to be gentle and patient.

If the world of obstetrics poses its pastoral problems, no less does the gynaecological ward where many of our parishioners will find themselves. Women are naturally reticent about the kind of operation they are going to have, and we shall be wise not to pretend to knowledge about these things even if we have it. Whether we like it or not, parsons are not supposed to know about such things! We ought to know about some of the effects on the whole system caused by the operation of hysterectomy: women are sometimes fearful that it will cause them to be no longer attractive in the eyes of their husbands. We should be able to reassure them.

In a ward where cases of induced abortion are frequently met, and where terminations of pregnancies, tying up of

Fallopian tubes, and other forms of sterilization are being performed every day, the young pastor straight from his theological college and his manuals of moral theology may be tempted to panic and rush out and shout about the murder of the innocents. It is true that grave moral problems do exist in this field, but we have to seek a solution elsewhere than by a hospital bed-side. We shall discuss this further in the chapter on medico-moral problems.

CHILDREN

A child's sick room or children's wards in a hospital are the most delightful of the places the priest goes to in the course of his visitations, and they need hold no terrors for the visiting minister if he remembers that any normal child (just like any adult!) wants to feel secure and wants to feel that he is respected as a person. An illness that causes real pain or brings the child into an unknown and strange environment, away from his family and people and things that he knows, is going to upset him. How often one sees, too, a child's physical condition deteriorating because of the manifest anxiety of a mother or relative.

A visit to a sick child, then, is as much to the parents as to the patient. This is the pastoral situation into which we enter when we come into the sick-room of a child or into the children's ward of a hospital.

The priest ought to extend further the feeling of security in the child's mind by his visit, which should be as "natural" as possible. This is not achieved by the minister indulging in childish prattle or by clowning in order to get laughs, but by respecting the child as a person.

For example, Simon is six years old. He is a "congenital heart case" and has to spend most of his life resting as he becomes breathless after only a few steps. He has been seen by cardiologists and cardiac surgeons, and it may be that when he is a little older the surgeons may decide to attempt an operation.

Despite his incapacity he is an intelligent boy with a restless mind. The Vicar calls on one of his periodical visits—

"Hello, Simon? How do you feel to-day?"

"Hello, Vicar. Mummy says I'm not so well and I have to stay in bed again."

"Bad luck, old boy. What have we got here?"

"This is my puzzle book. You have to fill in all these bits with a dot. Then you'll get an animal."

"I wonder what sort of an animal that one is?"

"I think it's going to be a seal."

"I like seals. Have you ever seen them on television?"

"Yes, the Blackpool one. Or perhaps the Billy Smart one last Christmas."

"I didn't see that one. I was in church, I think."

"Do you like going to church?"

"H'm . . . yes . . . mostly. Sometimes I don't."

"When don't you?"

"When it's cold outside and it's nice and warm inside and there's a good programme on the television!"

"But you have to go to take the service."

"Yes, it's my job."

"Daddy's a joiner. He made me a Noah's Ark."

"I like old Noah and the elephants."

"Was Noah real? Janice says he isn't."

"But the story's real. God told somebody to write it."

"Will God make me better? Mummy says so."

"God will help the doctors to make you better."

"Mummy says you're praying for me at church."

"Yes, we are—every day."

"Can God hear?"

"Yes—we can always talk to him wherever we are."

"Look, the Sunday School teacher sent me this card."

"Nice, isn't it. I'll come and see you again—God bless you."

We shall try to surround him with "security" and affection. Even when children are very ill indeed we ought to conceal our anxiety and fears. Death itself is treated in a very "matter-of-fact" way by children: we recall some very tense hours in a hospital children's ward when, despite hours and days of struggling for a child's life by medical and nursing staff, death came at 2.45 a.m. in the night. We had all become very fond of Johnny, and there were heavy hearts as everything was prepared for the removal of the body at 5 a.m. to the mortuary. We thought that our careful screening, our tip-toeing, our whispered directions had ensured that the rest of the sleeping ward would be undisturbed and would only see an empty bed in the morning. At 4.55 a.m. there came from a near-by bed a sibilant "Vicar, isn't it sad about poor Johnny?" One of his friends had lain quietly all night, listening to the movements and low voices of the doctors and nurses behind the screens. "But they did all they could—and he would never have got really better!" This from an eight-year-old who was not disturbingly precocious—who had a much more balanced attitude towards death than many an adult.

FOREIGNERS

It is interesting to speculate on what our Lord would have said and done if someone who did not speak his language had come for his help during his earthly ministry. We cannot doubt that he would have said and done something. It sometimes happens that we are called in to help someone who cannot speak English. It may be a sick refugee from Central Europe, a seaman who has fallen into the hold of his ship and broken both his legs, or a rich Greek who has been flown

F

in for a heart operation. The doctors and nurses will have taken steps to find an interpreter to help them in their task of diagnosis and treatment, but it is our duty to put them in touch with the appropriate priest or minister. It may be that we shall have to spend a great deal of time on the telephone to various Embassies and Consulates. Our pastoral concern for people will involve us in the sometimes tedious business of finding a Mohammedan mullah, or an Orthodox priest who can speak Russian, or a Lutheran pastor who knows how to deal with a Lithuanian. In the meantime, we have to make it clear to the patient that we are concerned as Christian pastors and to convey by sign language or by "pidgin" English that we are trying to convey the blessing of God to his condition. A young priest once found himself ministering to a dying Cypriot by pointing to words of comfort and reassurance in a Greek lexicon.

Perhaps it would be in place here to mention the importance of maintaining a happy liaison with ministers of other Churches and other religions. The world of sickness and the hospital ward is no place for the rivalries and attempts at proselytization which disfigure some parts of our religious life. Nor do we consider that a hospital is the appropriate sphere for the "plugging" of a particular line of churchmanship or belief. Difficulties there must always be, but in our experience the courtesy and co-operation which stem from mutual commitment in the task of ministering to the sick must always bring benefits to the person most concerned— the person in the bed.

PSYCHIATRIC CASES

It is not always realized that a great proportion of the hospital patients in this country is to be found in the hospitals for the mentally defective, the mentally ill, and the psychiatric case. The whole question of pastoral care for these patients is dealt with in a very competent manner in the Reverend Norman Autton's recent book *The Pastoral Care of the Mentally Ill,* and it is not our purpose to deal with this side of the priest's ministry. But one must always be on the alert to observe the signs of incipient mental disorder in one's patients. The cynical parish priest may say, "Half my people are bonkers, anyway", and may dismiss all "trick-cyclists" as godless and inept, but the wise priest will remember that mental illness is often something that can be cured as completely and effectively as pneumonia. He will also remember that psychiatric treatment should always be arranged through the general practitioner and not with some "Christian psychiatrist that he happens to know in London".

Many courses are arranged in different parts of the country for the clergy to learn more about psychiatry and pastoral clinical methods. Most of these are admirable and will help us to understand more fully the techniques of those who deal with mental disorders, and to make more effective our ministry to them, but we shall beware of the temptation to imagine ourselves as trained psychiatrists. If we are good pastors and really concerned for the welfare of our people, we shall not try to treat them ourselves, except in so far as by the ministry of Word and Sacrament we shall try to help them.

We know how irritating it is to be told by a cocksure psychiatrist, "Oh, *I* hear more confessions in a week in my consulting rooms than you do in a year in your church", and how amused he looks when the priest retorts, "Ah, but you can't give absolution". But surely the dialogue between priest and psychiatrist must lie at a much deeper level than this. And it will be so if we take pains to see that there is real consultation and co-operation between pastor and physician.

But the newly ordained priest who has to go to visit Mrs X in the County Mental Hospital may find this not very helpful. Hers may be a mental disorder of long standing; Mrs X has been in hospital for years and it seems hardly likely that she will ever return to her home. She started with what they called an "anxiety neurosis" and ultimately had to be taken away because she used to walk down the street in her night-dress and said some rather shockingly obscene things to the milkman.

The young priest's pastoral care of Mrs X will take the form of kindly, friendly visits. He will listen patiently to her rambling complaints, gently inquire about her spiritual welfare, and make certain that the Chaplain knows about her if she is a communicant, give her news about her friends and relatives, and in some cases give her a blessing before he leaves. He will be gentle but firm as he prepares to leave. He will have sought permission to go into her ward from the Sister or Staff Nurse on duty. The writer remembers vividly being embraced passionately by a patient who cried "Sanc-tuary—the Church" when she saw him; he could only get away by slipping out of his jacket and fleeing as the male nurses closed in on the patient. The inexperienced priest will be wise to seek the help and guidance of the staff.

BURNS UNITS

One Christmas Eve several years ago a hospital chaplain lay on the floor of a ward looking into the face of a girl who had been horribly burnt when her nylon nightdress caught fire. She had to be suspended in a special kind of framework face downwards. She received Holy Communion on Christmas morning but died soon afterwards. He cannot recall what words he said but he knew as he lay there that this was a situation in which God alone had something to give in the Sacrament of his Son's Body and Blood.

Many hospitals have special Burns Units where a constant high temperature is maintained and clothes need not be worn by the patients. Strict rules about masks and white coats for visitors have to be in force, and we shall be most careful about adhering to these rules. Badly burnt children, especially, are always very distressing cases, and we must never give any impression that we find the sight of such cases distasteful. The critical period for such cases lasts several weeks, and the parents or relatives need special care during the period of waiting.

VENEREAL DISEASE CLINICS

We are told that the rise in the rate of incidence of these diseases is startling, especially among young people. The moralist will make much of these figures, and the recent report of the B.M.A. on this subject has said many things that the Christian pastor will applaud. But if our pastoral duty brings us into contact with those who are suffering from these diseases it is important for us to remember that our ministry is much more that of a pastor than that of a judge.

As treatment is always confidential, it is unusual for there to be any kind of liaison or co-operation between priest and doctor except where a patient has expressed a desire for the help of a priest.

A Chaplain was visiting an Army V.D. Hospital in Batavia, in the Dutch East Indies, in 1946. The hospital was crowded with patients from all three services; disease was rife amongst the Eurasian women, and it was fairly safe to assume that most of the ailments which had brought the men to hospital had been contracted through liaisons in the bazaars and dance halls of the town.

Most of the men patients tried to be jocular about their presence—"It got them off convoy duty, anyway!"—and the Chaplain was wondering just what line he ought to take. He started talking to one young gunner who was lying on his bed reading. At first he protested a bit about his being in hospital at all. "I'm not like these others—it's not V.D. with me." The Chaplain never queried this although he had caught sight of the man's papers in the Orderly Room. Conversation wandered on—they talked about everything under the sun. At last the Chaplain rose to go. "Oh, by the way, that was all hooey about me not having V.D. Can I come and see you next week?"

The story was that he had gone out on a "blind" with his

friends after a spell on convoy duty. They had all drunk far
too much of the local "hooch" and all he could remember
was that he had found himself in a Eurasian girl's bed at
dawn the following morning. He had had to report sick some
weeks later and the M.O. had sent him into hospital. Underneath the bravado, he was deeply ashamed and felt that
he had betrayed his wife and the young child he had never
seen.

On his discharge from hospital, he sought out the Chaplain and made his peace with God through sacramental confession.

INFECTIOUS DISEASES

"Oh, priests don't catch diseases—they are immune." One
sometimes hears this arrogant remark by certain clergy who
try to spurn white coats and masks, and to by-pass the regu-
lations which "ordinary" people have to observe when visiting those who are suffering from infectious diseases: in hospital there are further rules about those who are "on barrier"
and the clergy can be an embarrassment to a young nurse
who is anxious to obey the orders of her superiors, if they
presume to be superior to her instructions.

Visits to patients suffering from poliomyelitis who are in
"iron lungs" should be short, and if it seems right to say
some prayers these should be concise and in the form of
ejaculations rather than of the rambling variety. The repeti-
tion of the words "Underneath are the everlasting arms" can
be of great help to patients who are paralysed and helpless.

Prayer cards or helpful pictures can be given, but we must
remember that pamphlets or loose papers are not practicable.
Large print is the best: sometimes the eyes do not focus very
well in serious illness.

When administering Holy Communion to patients who
are suffering from infectious diseases of any kind, it is always
preferable to use "intinction": indeed, it is the only method
practicable when the patient is lying down. The wafer is
touched with a little of the consecrated wine and the patient

receives Communion directly into the mouth. Further advice about this is given in the chapter on the administration of the Sacraments.

ACCIDENTS: CASUALTY WARDS

Not many Palm Sunday processions or distributions of palm crosses took place in the churches of the Rhineland in 1945. The Allied Armies had just crossed the Rhine and were engaged in the final offensive which led to VE day in May of that year. For one Army Chaplain that Palm Sunday began not with a commemoration of the Entry into Jerusalem at a palm-bedecked altar in a warm and comfortable parish church, but in the somewhat straitened conditions of a slit-trench just outside Wesel. After a distracting morning burying charred bodies of men whose gliders had been shot down the previous day, he transferred his pastoral activities during the afternoon to a Casualty Clearing Station which was a maelstrom of bustle and activity. It seemed to him that everybody knew what to do except himself.

"Padre, come here." The bewildered Temporary Chaplain to the Forces turned and sought, almost with relief, the man from whom the cry had come. He found an R.A.S.C. driver who had been blown up in his vehicle on a German anti-personnel mine, badly wounded, lying on a stretcher in a corner of the farm-house they were using as a C.C.S. It is difficult to conjure up exactly what the Chaplain expected would be required of him, but he *was* a little surprised when the man said, "Pass me that bowl, I want to spit."

Strangely enough, that request was the best introduction the raw chaplain could have had to battle-field technique. He proceeded to busy himself doing what he could in the situation in which he found himself.

Our behaviour as priests at the time of a serious accident must always be of the same kind. It can never be according to a pattern; an accident is, by its very nature, invariably unexpected. Spectators or members of the family, in their excitement and uncertainty, will probably overlook calling their pastor. He may hear about the accident in various ways; under the stress of such a situation many people become panicky, and we should not feel offended or unwelcome because we have not been called in.

In many situations, of course, he may be among the first to be told. He may have the task of ringing for the ambulance and the police (and please let us perfect our Dial 999 practice!), but, regardless of the way in which we become involved, our presence will always be appreciated by those who are affected by the accident.

The Casualty Department of any hospital has various examination rooms and treatment rooms together with waiting rooms for the relatives. Our task is to "father" the relatives, to give them confidence and courage through our presence and our concern, to act as a lubricant or liaison between them and the sometimes harassed medical and nursing staff; to do what we can for the injured one. If he is conscious, we can give him reassurance; if he is not conscious we can offer a silent prayer. If the doctor knows us and we know him, he will assess the situation for us, and we shall have some indication of how we ought to proceed. The important thing is for us to behave with calm and not to get in the way. There may not be time to bring the Last Sacraments; we should not get excited about this—there is always Spiritual Communion and surely God understands our predicament. Like the Army Chaplain, we do what we can.

THE MORTUARY

Consideration of death and our ministry to the dying and bereaved really falls outside the scope of this volume, but any priest's attempts to bring the consolations and comforts of the Christian religion ought to be seen *sub specie aeternitatis*. It is true that the pastor should emphasize the aspect of hope in his ministrations, hope of physical recovery and restoration to wholeness, but in some way we must always link that kind of earthly hope to the everlasting hope which embraces all the promises of Christ for faithful Christians when they have passed through the gate of death, as well as during this earthly pilgrimage.

The ease with which we have taken refuge in these last two sentences in the conventional language of the pulpit about the things of eternity will not blind us to the fact that such matters are not readily "understanded of the people"—even "our own people"—and patience with understanding is vitally necessary to us when we are asked questions about death and what the Church believes on the subject.

In the course of his ministry the parish clergyman will meet many situations when he has to face and deal with the sorrow, grief, disappointment, bitterness, bewilderment, and sometimes unreasoning behaviour of those who encounter the fact of death. It is desperately easy to apply the pious platitude to each case—"rest in the Lord" or "God's will" or "He's better off where he's gone" or "She's out of her suffering". The most important thing is to convey to the bereaved person one's real sympathy and compassion, and then to give what spiritual help is possible in the circumstances.

The priest is expected to know his way about unfamiliar processes such as the arrangement of funerals and the customs of his local undertaker and cemetery or crematorium. It is a good thing for the young priest to obtain permission to witness the actual process of the cremation of a body so that he is able to speak with knowledge when he is asked about the advisability of cremation in the case of death. Not seldom he is asked, too, about such questions as the giving of one's body for medical research after death or the removal of eyes for corneal grafting.

If he is asked to accompany people to the mortuary to identify a body or to see it after death, he should do so readily to give support to the relatives. In most cases the appropriate prayers to be said in the mortuary chapel will consist of Psalm 130, the Lord's Prayer, and the

Commendatory Prayer from the Visitation of the Sick in the Book of Common Prayer.

If a happy relationship has been established between the priest and the hospital staff, it is highly likely that he will be allowed to be present at a post-mortem examination. He will do this not only for the enlargement of his own experience, but in order that he may speak from knowledge when he is asked his advice about the giving of permission for a relative's body to be examined after death for purposes of medical research. In the same way, attendance at a surgical operation as a bystander will give the pastor confidence that he knows what he is talking about when discussing the prospect of surgery with a nervous patient.

In all these things the priest will find his capacity for "wonder" enlarged immeasurably. Many priests will remember the words of Bishop Geoffrey Lloyd at an Oxford Conference some years ago: "Wonder, like that of a child, would seem to be the basis of the life of a priest working in hospital or amongst the sick, and of all men we have need to bear constantly in mind our Lord's words 'Except ye become as little children, ye cannot enter the Kingdom of Heaven'. In other words, for our personality to make its mark in the ministry, we must aim at that simplicity and humility which is child-like but never childish."

This simplicity should bear fruit in the manner in which we become adaptable and flexible in our pastoral approach to people in all their differing situations, so that our ministry does not betray the marks of "text-book" or rule of thumb, but will win the accolade of "He's so adaptable".

9

Ministering to the Elderly

"I've had a good life."

There is a very unlovely word which has come into common usage during recent years to describe a facet of medical science which is not really new but which has had to be taken more seriously because of the dramatic growth in the number of older people in our midst—that word is "geriatrics". Our purpose is not to discuss this branch of medicine in detail, but to suggest to newly ordained pastors some of the factors which ought to be borne in mind when attempting a ministry to the ageing sick.

Further, we should be disloyal to our conviction that a priest should be concerned with the social situation in which a person under our care finds himself or herself, as well as the spiritual condition of our patient, if we did not consider one or two facts about the six million people over sixty-five in Britain at the present moment.

About a fifth of old people live alone. That does not mean that many of them do not prefer and like it. Most old people are in reasonably good health and most of them are in contact with relatives, friends, or neighbours.

It is probable that we shall be concerned with the four per cent of old people who are in institutions such as residential homes, hospitals, and nursing homes, or the one per cent (61,000) who are in psychiatric hospitals and nursing homes, together with the larger number who are ill at home.

If we digest these facts, for which I am indebted to the sociologist, Jeremy Tunstall, and his work on a national study of how old people live, we are more likely to see this part of our ministry in its proper perspective. Sometimes the impression is given that *all* old people are sick and suffering and unhappy; glib expressions like "the twilight of life" find their way into sermons; "the sick and aged suffering" intrude into public intercessions with sometimes a perceptible sigh; old age is often pictured as a tragedy.

There *are* great problems; there is much misery which could be alleviated by great developments in community care and a more realistic deployment of the medical services concerned with old people, but nothing should be encouraged by any agency, least of all the Church, which might take away from those who are growing old *their dignity*. We ought to applaud the unwillingness of an eighty-year-old widower to be dragooned into a "Darby and Joan Club" or "Evergreen Association" for old people, and we should salute his determination to preserve his independence and keep his home going. "What is the secret?" a man of ninety-eight was asked. "To have a purpose in life, my boy."

"THEY'VE PUT ME ON THE SHELF NOW"

The most important thing for the priest to remember in his ministry to old people is that they, like us, want affection, want to be recognized and to do something useful. However unattractive and incapable they have become, they are still children of God, and in all our ministrations we must recognize that. We may feel sometimes that some elderly people should be "preparing for death" rather than trying to do things more appropriate to a younger generation, but we must never reveal this!

The priest ought never to indulge in that kind of banter which is sometimes heard in institutions for old people, when nurses or attendants poke fun at slowly moving or very deaf people. "Come on, Gran, you'll be late for your funeral." Such remarks may be the cover for real affection and care, but it is unwise for the minister to say anything which would seem to indicate a lack of respect on his part for old age.

He should give the impression that as far as he and the Church are concerned, the patient has not been put on the shelf. Some old patients will value a request for them to share in the parish intercessions; they like to send their contribution to parish efforts and gift days and to hear about parish affairs if they have been members of a congregation.

The writer recalls one old patient who made it her task to intercede at different hours for all the people in the different streets of the parish. She was unable to hold a paper and so she made a mental map on the windows opposite her bed: "Olaf Street on the upper bar, Horsa Street on the down-piece, and so on. . . ."

CHRONIC DISORDERS

Memories and powers of concentration or attention become less acute with advancing years. The sense organs deteriorate: older people hear less well, see less well, and have, sometimes, a defective sense of taste. Food becomes tasteless even when a daughter or friend has lavished every possible culinary art on some special dish.

Even if there is no serious organic disease, aches and pains begin to make themselves felt more frequently, and everything seems to work more slowly. Most people in their seventies and eighties have to live with some chronic ailment or another. Ideally, the Christian pastor will help his people to accept these various handicaps without rebellion or hostility; in practice, it means we have to listen for a very long time to all the grumbles before we suggest that there is another side to the picture!

In some cases, our people can be encouraged to "live the liturgical life" by joining in the services of the Church through the reading of the service of Holy Communion, Mattins, and Evensong each day. This is perhaps possible only for the few, but the provision of a calendar or lectionary is often a great help to permanent invalids.

ADJUSTING TO OLD AGE

Most elderly people can adjust themselves and their mental outlook to the physical changes which are our common lot, but it is true that some become cynical and disgusted with themselves. They crave for attention and yet are most ungracious when they receive it; they become peevish and easily upset by things which people in middle age would never notice. To them it seems that life is passing them by, and they try to compensate for this by being ever more possessive about their sons and daughters and their grand-children. Anything that disturbs the routine of their lives or their comfort becomes an intolerable burden.

The pastor must be as patient as possible in dealing with these cases, and he must be prepared to spend a great deal of time just listening. He must be careful not to be drawn into a kind of alliance to defend the rights of the aged against the allegedly unjust and ungrateful son or daughter. We shall not allow ourselves to muse overmuch on the "tragedy of old age", but we ought to busy ourselves trying to help old people to grow old graciously.

RELIGIOUS MINISTRATIONS

The first thing we must realize is that older people are understandably fixed in their ways. Our ministry, therefore, ought to start with the things which are familiar to them. Well-known and well-loved hymns, well-known Bible passages form the basis of our approach. We have to speak slowly and audibly, adjusting our pace to their slower speed of thinking. If we suggest bringing the sacrament of Holy Communion, we have not to be disturbed if there is a lack of response; it may be that a good deal of gentle teaching will be necessary before the old person sees the need or cultivates a desire for the Blessed Sacrament.

The use of tape recordings of Church services in the sick-room has much to commend it, but arrangements should be made for somebody other than the priest to operate the machine—otherwise the clergyman may find that his whole day is taken up with mechanics.

If Bibles or Prayer Books are to be used, then they must have large print and a simple format. The "with-it" young priest should not be too anxious to introduce new translations, new interpretations, new ecclesiastical fashions! However right these may be for younger members of our congregations, it is doubtful whether they can be of great spiritual help to those who have been brought up for eighty years on one particular kind of spirituality.

THE PRIEST VISITS IN PART II ACCOMMODATION

This very odd nomenclature applies to the homes for old people which are run, not under the auspices of the Ministry of Health, but by the local authority. The Medical Officer of Health of the appropriate County or Borough Council is therefore the person ultimately responsible for their management.

We shall know such institutions as old folks' homes where there is usually a chaplain from the neighbouring parish who receives a nominal remuneration. He will normally conduct regular services and administer the sacraments; it is part of his "cure of souls".

Our visits to such places ought to be of an unhurried nature. We may have come to see one particular patient, but we should make friends, too, with all the residents. Our Christian approach to people ought not to be something which is switched on and off as we approach an individual patient.

The nurses, orderlies, and attendants in these homes need our ministry as well. They are often performing a much more wearing, though perhaps less spectacular, task of nursing than the young student nurse in a London teaching hospital; they have to deal with old patients who are unattractive and sometimes unreasonable in their demands. Very frequently they are "part-time" and have a home and family to run in addition to their duties in hospital. They will welcome our visits and any assistance we can give in making their charges' lives more pleasant with organized visiting by young wives' clubs, carol singers, and choirs.

One of the disquieting things about life in an old people's home is the speed with which people can become anchored to a kind of institutional inactivity; routine leads to a deadly inertia which causes them to allow their mental and bodily muscles to harden, so that life develops into a boredom which results in a cantankerous, cabbage-like existence. We should do what we can to encourage any kind of cultural or recreational interests.

The Welfare Officer of the local authority is someone whose friendship and co-operation we ought to cultivate where these matters are concerned.

HOSPITALS FOR
MENTALLY DEFECTIVE PATIENTS

"Oh, I never go in there; there's no point." The clergyman was speaking of the acute ward in the mental block of his local hospital. It must be confessed that it often seems that visiting the mentally defective (as opposed to the mentally sick) is unprofitable, and many a priest has asked himself after spending half an hour amongst a roomful of mentally defective patients, "Have I done any good?"

We would suggest that this is the wrong question to ask oneself. We ought to go as ambassadors of Christ to wherever our people are—to prison cell or padded room. The fact of our visit and our presence has its effect on the patient, even though our words follow a pattern which bears little resemblance to the contorted images which fill our hearer's mind.

It has been found that familiar words and familiar actions

(for example, the receiving of Holy Communion) do elicit a response even from those who are most mentally disturbed. So we must always persevere with our visiting in these wards, always taking the advice of the nursing staff and the medical officers.

Senility amongst the elderly is distressing, but we can reassure relatives that it has physical causes and does not reflect on their care. Despite all the intensive education of the population about mental health, most people still think that there is something disgraceful about mental troubles.

THEN COMES THE END

An old lady of eighty-two who worshipped in church with great regularity was taken ill and had a very serious heart attack, being unconscious for some days. The priest was called; he said prayers for the commendation of her soul and anointed her. The family were told by the doctor that there was no hope of recovery, and provisional arrangements were made for the funeral.

She made a startling recovery and in a week or two was out and about again. "Eh!" she said, "God won't have any gi'en stuff." It took some little time for the priest to comprehend this piece of pawky wisdom. . . . "But I've had a good life and I shan't complain when God takes me."

This is the kind of dignified attitude towards old age that Church and community should foster in all ministries to the elderly. Not for Christians surely the concept of Shakespeare's "lean and slippered pantaloon", but the robust counselling of Cicero's *De Senectute*: "Mature fieri senem si diu velis senex esse."

Death sometimes takes place in squalor and bewilderment, but in our ministry we must try to preserve the dignity which is the right of any human soul as it approaches the mystery of death; in the "sure and confident hope of the Resurrection to eternal life through our Lord Jesus Christ" may these

G

words be said by priest, nurse, or relative as our people leave this life:

> Go forth upon thy journey from this world,
> O Christian soul,
> In the name of God the Father Almighty, who created thee. Amen.
> In the name of Jesus Christ who suffered for thee. Amen.
> In the name of the Holy Spirit who strengtheneth thee (sanctified thee at thy baptism). Amen.
> In communion with the blessed Saints, and aided by Angels and Archangels, and all the armies of the heavenly host. Amen.
> May thy portion this day be in peace, and thy dwelling in the heavenly Jerusalem. Amen.

IO

Clergy—Doctor Co-operation

"I suppose you would say that that is how God works."

A few years ago at three o'clock one October afternoon a
priest was administering Holy Communion and the sacrament of Holy Unction to a patient who was considered by
her doctors and friends to be dying. There had been a certain
amount of reorganization on the part of the Ward Sister
because it was an afternoon for one of the Consultants' teaching rounds. As the priest came into the ward he found the
screens drawn round the patient's bed, the rest of the ward
was very still and quiet, and the Consultant was quietly
teaching his firm of house officers and students in a distant
corner of the ward near the kitchen.

One of the House Physicians watched the priest carefully
as he went behind the screens; this patient was his special
concern and he had talked that morning with the pastor
about what *he* was going to do. He had been deeply interested in the details of the ministry which the Chaplain was
purposing for "his" patient.

Although very weak and bordering on the unconscious the
patient was able to realize the meaning of the short service
and to join in the Lord's Prayer, before lapsing into a coma.

Two days later there were signs of a distinct recovery and
very soon the patient was helping the staff to take round the
meals. The priest met the House Physician in the ward.

"X is remarkably better, isn't she?"

"Yes, I'm so glad," said the priest. "You've done a good
job."

"Er—yes. Do you know—that day you did *your* stuff—I'd
changed the drug that morning?"

"Well, actually I did know. The Sister told me."

There was a long silence. Both men realized that they were each waiting for the other to claim a success for their own brand of "medicine". But the young doctor suddenly saw the point.

"I suppose you would say that that is how God works."

"I suppose it is", said the priest.

It is a commonplace that Church and Medicine have long been partners and that our modern hospitals had their beginnings in the guest-houses and sick-rooms of religious institutions of the Middle Ages. We can point to the title of "Sister" as a reminder of the religious origin of nursing care.

But sometimes it would seem that the Church is more anxious to claim the world of medicine as a partner than the medical world is to acknowledge us! It may be true that at one point in history religion and medicine went hand in hand, but the humanist doctor can quite rightly point to the more ancient foundations of his craft in Greece or Egypt.

It is a sad thing that there has been a divorce between Medicine and the Church, but sometimes we give the impression that we are bewailing it without admitting our share in the mistakes which led up to it. The Church is certainly not the innocent party.

One of the reasons for the break-up of the marriage was the tendency of the Church to emphasize unduly the kind of doctrinal teaching which regards the body or physical nature of man as inherently evil and the soul alone as capable of redemption. When the Church persisted in its views and refused to acknowledge some of the findings of medical science, it caused the medical profession to go into isolation.

At the same time the claims of some medical scientists that they had all the answers, and that the Church had nothing to offer to sick and diseased except comfort and consolation, were a source of intense irritation to ministers of all denominations.

But we can be thankful that the tide has turned, and it is no exaggeration to say that the breach is beginning to be healed. But we have a very long way to go!

We should like to consider now some of the aspects of the situation the newly ordained may find in his first parish.

PRE-ORDINATION CO-OPERATION

He will be fortunate if his theological college has included any course of lectures on clergy–doctor co-operation. In a tiny minority of cases he will have been present at perhaps a brief conference organized for medical and theological students on such subjects as "Disease". It is more than likely that he will have listened to a lecture or a talk on mental disturbance and illness by a visiting doctor. There is a small chance that he may have been to a systematic, six-week course at St George's Hospital, London, or at Guy's Hospital. Again, he *may* have been on a part-time course extending over three terms at Littlemore Hospital.

The emphasis is most likely to have been on mental health and psychiatry, in which, it has been suggested, theological students have an almost unhealthy interest, and it is doubtful whether the subject of medical science will have received any more attention in the ordinand's course than the work of moral welfare, the duties of a probation officer, and the outline of trades union organization.

The Theological College principal will quite understandably speak of curricula which are groaning at the seams. What then is suggested? We suggest more joint seminars for medical and theological students where both kinds of students may learn more about one another's mental disciplines, where theologians may lecture on the Christian aspect of healing, and where experts in the different branches of medicine may expound the different methods of diagnosis, scientific analysis, and treatment. So would both sides grow together in their thinking from ground level.

This is not entirely new. F. D. Maurice used to give a

course of lectures on moral philosophy to medical students at Guy's Hospital in 1838, and we understand that Mr Hugh Arthur has arranged lectures for theological students in Newcastle during recent years.

It is sad, but our final observation in this section must be that of the Working Party on Clergy–Doctor Co-operation set up by the Archbishop of Canterbury in April 1962: "Our conclusion, therefore, about the training of theological students and medical students in those aspects of their vocation in which co-operation is called for, is that the surface of these questions has not yet even been scratched."

CO-OPERATION IN THE PARISH

When the ordinand has completed his theological college course, has been ordained, unpacked his books, and become settled in a parish, he will go out and visit his people. Some of them will be sick, some of them will be in hospital, many of them will be in need of the care of a doctor. What will the young minister find in the way of liaison or co-operation between the worlds of practical medicine and pastoral theology?

The evidence points to the fact that work in this field, too, can scarcely be said to have begun. "Great strides have been made by the Clinical Theology Association, under the able guidance of Dr Frank Lake, to provide more systematic training for the clergy. But this initiative, valuable and important though it is, does not contribute directly to the furtherance of the mutual work of doctors and clergy, because the primary aim of the Clinical Theology courses is to equip parish clergy with greater skills in the handling of cases of psychiatric disorder and difficulty—to effect, if possible, the cure of pathological conditions encountered and by this activity to contribute also to prevention." (Report to the Archbishop of Canterbury.)

The Working Party was able to trace about fifty-five clergy–doctor groups which are meeting more or less regularly in different parts of the country. If the young priest has been ordained in the Diocese of Newcastle he is much more likely to encounter one of these groups than in any other diocese as, apparently, sixteen of them are in that diocese.

But there is no central organization and no means of communication between the groups. On the whole, the discussions in such groups would seem to be about case-book situations and are slanted heavily towards the psychiatric and psycho-somatic aspects of illness. This is a most fruitful type of approach and the Church would do well to foster this kind of discussion group.

The Report goes on: "The Working Party's sphere of interest is where the clerical and medical disciplines overlap —where they can best work together. Our objective is that Church and people should be served by priests and doctors who are fully aware that in the attainment and preservation of health of the whole man, body, mind, and spirit are interdependent, and that the specific skills which members of one or other of these interdependent parts possess can be greatly enriched by more appreciation of and understanding of the skills of the other."

Some suggestions are made in the Report about future lines of action. A "College of Religion and Medicine" is envisaged, and the establishment of diocesan consultative services on medico-pastoral relations, where clergy and doctors could get advice and help on how to deal with the medical and spiritual problems they encounter.

All this is of vast importance, and much will have to be done along these lines, but what about the new curate at St Millicent's and Mr Jones? Remember him? He's in Bed No. 22.

THE PARISH PRIEST
AND THE G.P.

In many a country parish the local doctor and the parson are close personal friends; the doctor may be Rector's Warden and read the lessons; there is complete *rapport* where the villagers are concerned in regard to their ailments both spiritual and physical. The Vicar's dilapidated shooting-brake may be the only means of transport for visitors to the local hospital; the dates of opening for the village clinic will be published in the parish magazine, and the District Nurse's holiday arrangements will be found amongst the notices about the Flower Show on the church notice-board. The country parishes may not be in the forefront in regard to the introduction of new liturgies, but they show an instinctive understanding of what the Incarnation really means by an unembarrassed acceptance of the fact that their Church calendar includes racing fixtures as well as "O Sapientia".

In the larger conurbations (country parsons have some-times read the Paul Report) co-operation with the doctor may be more difficult. In a large parish there will of course be many general practitioners; the territorial boundaries of their practices will not be coterminous with parish bounda-ries, and it may be that the doctor who treats most of our parishioners will live in somebody else's parish. There will be excuses galore for our not making contact with him; we may have been put off by being told that Dr O'Flaherty is a militant R.C. or that Dr Smith is an agnostic who pours scorn on "religious" patients; perhaps we become nettled when his dispenser tells us that if we want to see him it will have to be during surgery hours.

Whatever the difficulties (and surely there are difficulties about most pastoral problems!) we ought to make the great-est efforts to cultivate a friendly relationship with all the doctors who have anything to do with the people in our parishes. We should never be afraid of going to them and asking if we might discuss Mr Jones's illness and matters concerning it. We shall find that doctors are often as shy of us as we are of them.

What we would suggest here is that the shepherd's task—the pastoral office as it is known in the Church—is something that is not confined to the ordained ministry. Rather is it a focalization of a function of the whole Christian community and its members. Every one of us exercises influence on other people, not least the medical man. *We share the pastoral care of Mr Jones with Doctor X*, because every one of us who calls himself a Christian, and indeed those who do not, shares in the ministry of Christ. We shall distort and maim the Christian Gospel if we claim that only the clergy have a responsibility for caring pastorally—in a shepherd-like way—for people.

The priesthood is something that is very dear to us as ministers of the Gospel, but there *is* a sense in which all believers share in the priesthood of Christ and the pastoral duties of that priesthood.

A doctor's share is a very great one. He is dealing with human beings, with individuals, at great crises in their lives, just as a priest or minister is. He can influence them for good or ill. In many cases, the priest to-day has become envious of the trust which many patients have in their doctors—the medical practitioner is entrusted with far more secrets and confidences than many a parish priest—to a great extent the surgery *has* become a confessional despite our justified protestations. What a high and weighty office this is to which a *doctor* is called.

There is abundant evidence that doctors do not treat lightly this responsibility, but it is equally evident that seldom do they have time for dealing with all that is involved. When we complain (as there is no doubt we shall!) about the "overworked clergy" let us remember the occasions we have had supper, perhaps, with a general practitioner who has been "on call" and marvelled at the patience with which he has dealt with call after call on his telephone. The doctor has much to teach us!

The fact that there is sometimes a grave lack of co-operation in the pastoral task of the Church where sickness is concerned is due to the fault of no particular side. The clergy are as jealous of their professional interests as the doctor is of his own. Both sides are apt to take refuge in a sort of *mystique* which surrounds theology as well as medicine. Both sides rejoice in their jargon in the same way that lawyers encompass their calling with archaisms and traditions which bemuse the ordinary person.

WHERE WE CAN START

What would seem to be needed *now* is not yet another pattern of committees to discuss ways of co-operation between doctor and priest, but a real effort on the part of both clergy and medical men, in any locality, to become friends. In our experience, far more is done over a cup of tea or a glass of sherry in the doctor's house or vicarage to establish understanding and friendly relations between the worlds of religion and medicine than in any other way. We learn how each other "ticks", how each other does his job, we learn more about the mental disciplines which steer our thinking.

And let it be said that no doctor need fear that by co-operating with the clergy he will be guilty of the technical offence of associating with an unqualified practitioner. Following the statement by the B.M.A. in 1947, co-operation is to be encouraged, and the doctor, with the patient's consent, should extend the same courtesy to his clerical colleague as he does to his medical colleagues, giving the relevant details of the case he is referring (B.M.J. Supplement, 1947, Vol. II, p. 112, 8 November).

It need hardly be said that a comparable responsibility rests on us. We often come across disease long before the doctor is called in. Our sick ministry ought to be preventive as well as curative.

TO WHAT PURPOSE?

At the end of 1948 the writer was asked with some asperity by a somewhat aloof dignitary of the Church, "So you are one of these people who try to work with doctors? You're always talking about co-operation, but what do the doctors expect? No medical man has ever asked me for *my* co-operation."

We can be thankful that such an attitude is much less in evidence, but some people will still ask querulously, "To what purpose is all this talk?" The purpose of it surely is that the *total* ministry of the Church—priest, doctor, nurse, almoner, . . . may be brought to bear on the calamities which afflict the body and soul of Mr Jones and others of Christ's sheep which are scattered abroad.

The purpose of it all is not that the Reverend Jones may become an amateur medical practitioner or a pseudo-psychiatrist. We have seen some of the disastrous effects of teaching the clergy a *little* psychiatry, and we have learned with dismay of clergy in the United States who have become so bogged down with reading case histories and being concerned with diagnosis that they rarely have time to visit and care for their people. Pastoral care is more than counselling, is more than just sitting in the confessional for hours on end, although, of course, *it may well include this*.

No! The purpose of it all is that the pastoral work of the Church may be done with greater efficiency. The true pastor cares for his sheep with a devotion even to the death; he knows them and is known by them. This is the key to that work of the Church which embraces both doctor and priest in their care for Mr Jones (now convalescing). God's Ministry of Healing is one which overlaps with, and indeed comprehends, the Ministry of Health.

This quotation from Archbishop Temple's *Readings in St John's Gospel* would seem to apply with equal force to the life and purpose of the Vicar and Dr So-and-so down the road: "It is not by what we say that we are good pastors, nor by what we do; but by what we are. And we are poor sheep like those whom we would tend. The one hope is that as folk come to know us they find in fact another—not the sheep turned shepherd, but in truth the Good Shepherd."

II

Medico-Moral Problems

"Does it work?"

In any discussion of parish techniques at normal clerical gatherings the most frequent question to be heard after the Rector of Little Blowing-on-the-water has described some parochial innovation which it is hoped will revolutionize the spiritual life of that little hamlet, is "But does it work?" The answer is: Yes, it has quite often doubled the congregation and trebled the Free Will Offerings in other parishes. It is only when the rapturous comments have died down that the very scholarly incumbent of Great Bracenbit gently casts doubts on the theological propriety of what his brother at Little B. proposes to do.

Not infrequently the impression is given that the "dialogue" between the Church and medical science follows much the same course. Medical science has discovered or perfected some technique which works successfully, and the Church, not always with sufficient justification but often rightly anxious about certain principles of moral theology, has drawn attention to another side of the picture.

This dialogue will always go on: we must always be ready to welcome developments in medicine and surgical techniques, but at the same time we must reserve the right to make critical assessments and apply Christian insights to the findings and achievements of medical science. But please may those assessments be informed assessments!

THERE ARE CERTAIN PRINCIPLES

Those who are experts in moral theology will remind us that not everything which is possible is necessarily right. In a world where "success" is often the main criterion of human endeavour there is a common tendency to suppose that because human ingenuity has made it possible to achieve a certain result, then that result ought to be achieved.

The moral theologian will also remind us that "the end does not necessarily justify the means". Those engaged in the treatment and healing of disease are especially prone to make the mistake of assuming that the end *does* justify the means. Our medical friends may be utterly devoted to their important task of healing disease, and it must seem to them that anything which enables them to achieve their aim must be right. It *is* possible to produce the right end, such as healing obviously is, by the wrong means.

Another consideration which should guide our thinking, especially in regard to the question of pain-killing drugs for dying people, is what the theologians call the Law of Double Effect. This lays down that it is only lawful to perform an action, one or more of the results of which are seen to be bad, provided that the action itself in its object or immediate effect is a right action.

EUTHANASIA

"But surely the kind thing would be to put him out of his pain, Vicar." We shall often meet this kind of plea from relatives who have spent days and nights at the bed-side of someone who is in the terminal stages of, say, cancer. We may be tempted to think that it would be a merciful act on the part of the doctor to inject a lethal amount of morphine in order to hasten death, but we have to remember that the medical man is bound by his Hippocratic oath and we ought to ask ourselves, "Kind to whom?"

There are those who are very active in the promotion of the aims and objects of the Euthanasia Society and their activities are prompted by very worthy ideals, but as Christian pastors we cannot support them.

However, it should be remembered that it can hardly be

considered a Christian duty for relative, doctor, or nurse to *prolong the act of dying*. Unreasonable efforts to prolong the life of someone who is drawing near to death are not demanded by Christian moral principles. Nor are pain-killing drugs which are likely in the long term to shorten life to be condemned.

ABORTION AND
TERMINATION OF PREGNANCIES

It is very unlikely that the parson in his parish will be acquainted with the enormous number of "illegal" abortions which are taking place daily in our midst. "Natural" abortion is something that very often *does* come into the pastoral scene. By this term is meant that for some reason or another the foetus is expelled from the mother's womb before the twenty-eighth week of gestation. Sometimes it recurs in pregnancy after pregnancy. This is a medical problem and no moral considerations are involved, but often the parents are longing to have children and we have to help the would-be mother in all the ways we can. Disappointment has to be transmuted into new resolve and the Sacraments often do what we cannot do with our attempts at verbal comfort.

What we have to try to tell such disappointed patients is that abortion or miscarriage is often nature's way of rejecting a mal-formed foetus, but that this does not mean it must always be so with future pregnancies.

We have to be patient, too, with the emotional disturbances which often follow a miscarriage. This is usually due to the hormonal imbalance which is caused, and husbands have to be reassured about this.

"Induced abortion" is the illegal kind; legally, in this country, it is an offence to procure, or to attempt to procure, abortion, and it is punishable by a severe sentence of imprisonment. The sentence laid down is not less than three years' penal servitude and can be for life. In reality, the criminal abortionist is charged with murder.

We shall be very careful not to apply this kind of police court language to those for whom we have care; nor does it seem to us to be entirely accurate to equate abortion with murder. But there would appear to be no doubt about the fact that we must never condone the act of abortion, however much we may sympathize with the reasons which have led the person concerned to seek this easy way out.

Perhaps we shall feel the inequity of the situation which prevails—the police do not take proceedings against reputable gynaecological surgeons, who have operated to procure abortion in the interests of the mother's life, nor against less reputable surgeons who have operated for less worthy motives, whereas they do prosecute the unqualified abortionist. We shall do well to ascquaint ourselves with the dangers of criminal abortion in the back streets, because we shall often meet the results in the gynaecological ward of our local hospital.

Before taking up a "judgemental" attitude towards any case that we may meet, we should recall to our minds the circumstances in which most of these illegal operations take place. There is a secrecy which cloaks the proceedings and the woman is in a tense, emotional state; thus, the danger of shock is increased and the manipulations of the abortionist made more difficult. The operation is often done in haste and the abortionist often fails to guard against infection. There is little after-care; the woman is left to her own devices and if complications ensue, she is often gravely ill before medical aid is called.

When the case comes into the care of the doctor there is another nice problem. The responsibility of reporting the case to the authorities rests with him, and the doctor is faced with a conflict of interests. He has a moral obligation to respect the confidence of his patient and, therefore, disclosure of the fact that she has been the subject of criminal abortion can be made only with her consent. This conflicts with the doctor's duty in law; any act or omission which conceals a felony is an offence. It is common practice, however, for the medical practitioner not to report these cases to the police unless the patient should die. In this case he is unable to certify the death as being due to natural causes and the death must be reported to the coroner.

"LEGAL" ABORTION

The unpleasant associations of the word "abortion" have led to the more common use of the more unwieldy phrase "termination of pregnancy", but it would be difficult to find legal justification for any such operation as the law at present stands, apart from the principle stated in the well-known case of Rex *v*. Bourne in 1939.

But these terminations do take place, and it is highly likely that we shall be asked about the propriety of the operation either by the mother or by a surgeon undecided about a particular case. There would seem to be little doubt that the moral theologian would consider that an abortion induced because of organic disease in the mother is justifiable on Christian grounds, but that an abortion induced on the grounds of psychiatric disease in the mother is less easy to justify.

We must be guided by the principles enunciated earlier in this chapter as to what we say; the difficult task of assessing the mother's bodily and mental health and the possible effects of pregnancy and labour upon her health is imposed on the doctor; if he looks for guidance about the moral aspect of the case, we ought to be able to give it. But it would be difficult to find any hard-and-fast rule laid down by our Church.

What we hope and pray for is that other therapeutic advances may eventuate which will make unnecessary any procurement of abortion for organic diseases. But the psychiatric cases will remain!

THE PROBLEMS OF
NEURO-SURGERY

"But this is what Hitler did with his political prisoners—
let his doctors play about with their brains!" And that, for
some people, is the last word on the subject of psycho-
surgery. Such an attitude is not of much help to the neuro-
surgeon who is often very exercised in mind and spirit about
the rightness of the operations he is called upon to perform.
We should reflect, too, that any kind of surgery was at one
time condemned by the Church because it represented an
attack on the physical nature of a human being. (The following may be irrelevant, but it is interesting to note that
even blood-tests of race horses are not allowed to be taken in
suspected "doping" cases because that would constitute a
contravention of the law of trespass, whereas Mr Jones in
Bed No. 22 is subjected to every kind of blood-test and
injection!¹)

It would be helpful, perhaps, for us to remember that the
operation of leucotomy—the inflicting of damage on the
frontal part of the brain—has been practised for only just
over twenty years. Those who are most skilled in this field
will admit that many mistakes have been made, but would
plead that it is a mistake to approach the subject emotion-
ally; that it is unhelpful to condemn the process outright,
and that those concerned with faith and morals should try to
see what it has to offer and give support to those who are
working to replace this operation with something better.

"But does it work?" The answer is yes in most cases. But
then one still has to answer the question whether anyone
has the right to tamper with a person's personality by means
of surgery. Leucotomy does rid people of gross obsessions
but in many cases it does often induce an attitude of in-
dolence. It may make people easier to live with but at the
same time less interesting and lovable. And if "tampering
with anyone's personality" sounds like another emotional

¹ Although, of course, he is legally *entitled* to object.

H

description of a very responsible department of surgery, we have to remember that those who undergo this operation are usually people whose personality is already deranged to a considerable degree. One might say they have already been "tampered with" by "nature".

The pastor will try to bear all these considerations in mind as he tries to advise those who approach him on this subject.

TELLING A PATIENT THE TRUTH

This is a question which very frequently crops up when clergy meet to discuss their dealings with sick people. It usually concerns those who are dying or have been found to be suffering from an incurable disease. Ought they to be told?

The seemingly unsatisfactory answer is: It all depends on the person involved, their circumstances, their relatives' wishes, their own spiritual maturity, and—the doctor. The doctor will know far better than the priest ever can know what the prognosis of any particular person's ailment may be. To him alone belongs the right to say to a patient, "Medical knowledge has enabled us to do whatever can be done in your case, but it seems to me that your disease is incurable by any means known to me."

But, it will be asked, what should a priest say if the patient asks him outright, "Am I going to die?" Our reply should be on these lines: "That is a question I am not qualified to answer—I am not a doctor; but if it should be true, I do not think there is anything to be frightened of—and we must all die sometime. We are all dying men throughout our lives, really." We should never tell a patient an untruth. He will cease to trust us. But sometimes it is better not to tell the *whole* of the truth at once. Experienced doctors will agree that patients who die slowly always eventually know and accept it just as do the aged.

To many a young priest beginning his ministry to sick people there does seem to exist a conspiracy of silence amongst doctors and nurses which is apparently aimed at deceiving the patient about his or her real condition. He will become impatient and complain that he is hampered in his work of helping patients to prepare for death. Let him be patient a little longer and he will discover that many doctors *do* tell their patients the truth when they think that the right moment has come and they consider the patient to be of the temperament which will be able "to take it". When he talks wildly of losing the opportunity of bringing a person to make a death-bed repentance, let him reflect that no less a person than Archbishop Heenan has publicly said that he has never known of such a case in his ministry.

The writer has been privileged to be present on more than one occasion when a doctor has told a patient gently and compassionately that there is no hope for him and has left the priest to speak of a much larger hope. This is really our task.

We speak of "preparing a person for death", but it is sometimes to be wondered whether we claim too much for our ministry. The manner of life and the religious beliefs of any person are really his preparation for the last moments of his life. *Our* skills are necessary for the assistance of the individual to use whatever light God has vouchsafed to him during his earthly pilgrimage.

We have discussed only some of the medico-moral problems which arise in the ministry of both doctor and pastor. Questions about sterilization, contraception, artificial insemination, and the like will no doubt exercise our minds, and we must refer the reader to the expert treatises on these subjects which have come from the pens of competent writers in recent years.

We humbly suggest that the young minister should read widely on these subjects before laying down the law. There is a wide range of easily read literature on these subjects; some of it is well informed and helpful, but we should

H*

beware of the hysterical pamphlets on Birth Control still to be found in back-street Dublin churches. To some the whole idea of artificial insemination is "revolting, repugnant, repulsive, and repellent". But we ought to have something positive to say; recently a doctor asked us if the fact that male semen could now be obtained by electrical stimulation of the prostate gland had made any difference to the Catholic objection to A.I.H. We found it difficult to answer.

In all these matters we ought to bear in mind the considerations which we suggested that the moral theologian brings before us at the beginning of this chapter. Further, we shall remember that we are called to take part in a very important task—the reconciling work of the Church in correlating medical ethics which have as their basis the welfare of the patient with Christian morals which have their root in the revelation of God.

12

Total Healing

> Because I believe in the Incarnation
> [said a great saint], I MUST be interested
> in the Report of the Local Sewage Board.[1]

Because the pastor is concerned with the body, mind, and spirit of his sick charge, he will be interested in, and concerned about, the whole range of healing agencies which are available to "the sick and impotent of the parish". We ought not to despise any opportunity of learning about, and co-operating with, any of the manifold services and therapeutic aids which are accessible to our people.

Canon Stanley Evans has written in his book *The Church in the Back Streets* of his vision of the parish pastor as being in part a social group worker who leads by assisting his pastoral charges to become, under the inspiration of the Holy Spirit, friendly societies based upon love and mutual aid. He envisages many of the unused churches in our large towns being, as it were, clearing-houses for the dissemination of information about the welfare services, which have been designed to help towards that "total" healing which doctor, priest, district nurse, psychiatrist, welfare officer, and local community can achieve together. The busy parish priest will no doubt throw up his hands in horror at such ideas: he will remind us of the "true nature" of the Church and of the aberrations of "social Christianity" in the past. We shall be reminded that the parish clergyman already has his hands full with his daily services, his prayers, his visiting, and administration of the sacraments. We may even be reminded of the ordination service where we promised to "lay aside the study of the world and the flesh".

[1] Roger Lloyd, *Revolutionary Religion.*

But we also promised that in our ministry we would "maintain and set forwards quietness, peace, and love, among all Christian people, and especially among them that are or shall be committed to our charge". Quietness, peace, and love are inextricably bound up with that ministry to the whole of life—man's spiritual, physical, and mental welfare —which we believe the Ministry of Healing to be.

In our parish work we ought to try to maintain friendly liaison and co-operation with some, if not all, of these contributors to the total healing of our people.

THE DISTRICT NURSE

"I'm afraid you can't come then with Communion; you see, the District Nurse always comes at that time." We may feel irritated until we reflect that the District Nurse's visit is as much Christ's "cup of cold water" as our visit is to bring Christ's nourishing and healing grace through the Blessed Sacrament. She may know far more about our patients than we do; sometimes she is the recipient of confidences to a far greater extent than we are ever permitted to be; she can be of enormous assistance to us if we seek her co-operation.

WELFARE OFFICERS AND HOME HELPS

Often the only way that sick and elderly people are able to continue an independent existence in their own homes is by having a "home help" to do their domestic cleaning and minor shopping. This service is organized by the local authority and the general practitioner knows the routine for obtaining their help: the loneliness, fear, and worry which are to be found in some ill patients should be shared and borne by all of us.

W.V.S. AND MEALS ON WHEELS

Dr R. A. Lambourne, in his remarkable book *Community, Church and Healing*, writes that

the visitation of the sick is the declaring and making present of the whole Christ. It is indeed a Church occasion, but it is only so by the loving response of the people of God to the sickness situation in their midst. This loving response of the people of God is the love of the fellowship (*koinonia*), which will be manifested in healing and preaching, and manifested in spiritual acts such as the giving of cups of water, injection of penicillin, or construction of hygienic latrines.

In the same way, we should see the visit of the voluntary worker twice a week to the lonely Mrs M, who can only move with difficulty between her bed, her chair, her gas stove, and her commode, is a real part of the Visitation of the Sick as cheap, well-cooked meals are brought round; those who do this work have realized how it is often the visits rather than the food which are welcomed and appreciated.

DISTRICT MIDWIVES AND HEALTH VISITORS

Here again we can make invaluable contacts. It has to be admitted that very often these members of the caring community do not enjoy the publicity or the status which the clergy sometimes achieve, but they may very well know the difficulties and ailments of our parishioners better than we do. We have known cases of lapsed communicants being recovered, people brought into the worshipping fellowship of the Church, and moral problems sorted out through the ministry of midwives and health visitors.

FAMILY PLANNING ASSOCIATIONS

It is realized that many priests will have mental reservations on the subject of Birth Control, but it should be remembered that advice is available to everybody regardless of religious affiliation. Those who can only accept the "rhythm" method of family planning will receive sympathetic help, and a great deal of work has been done in regard to sub-fertility. No matter how expert we think ourselves on these subjects, we should never hesitate to put our people in touch with those who have been trained in these matters.

THE ALMONERS

In his contacts with members of his congregation who have gone into hospital, the parish priest will often have to seek the advice and help of the Almoner. We must never think of this integral part of the hospital "healing team" as a department concerned solely with the dispensing of financial help and the arrangement of accommodation at convalescent homes. The Institute of Almoners is a highly professional body with strict standards of training; their standard of professional ethics is equally high, and confidence and trust between priest and almoner must be well established before there can be complete co-operation.

These are only some of the agencies with which we must establish liaison for the sake of the parish priest's sharing in the total care of our people. "When men and women through the faithful witness of the Church see the clinical event and the administrative act for welfare and healing as the works of Christ, and when they acknowledge them as such and, like the tenth leper, fall on their knees and offer a Eucharist to God for what he has done, then has salvation come upon them."[1]

[1] R. A. Lambourne, op. cit.

13

The Administration of the Sacraments to the Sick

"Do you think it will do me good?"

At first sight it may seem a little strange that the part of the priest's ministry which can be performed by him only—the administration of Holy Communion, Unction, and the hearing of confessions—should be left until the last chapter in this book. "I get bored with visiting and ringing up the district nurse, but I really *enjoy* taking the sacraments to people", said a young curate. Of course, we believe that sacramental religion is important and that administering the Blessed Sacrament is an essential part of our task; otherwise we should not have denied ourselves so much sleep, in common with many other hospital chaplains, in taking the Eucharist to hundreds of patients in hospital beds "very early in the morning, while it was yet dark".

But we feel that it is only when we see the giving of the sacraments as the culmination and the focalization of the caring Church's loving ministry of healing that we shall see our task as priests in its right perspective.

When we suggest to Mr Jones, in bed at home, waiting for the Consultant to come and give his verdict, that we might bring him Holy Communion at home, his first question, whether spoken or unspoken, is "Do you think it will do me good?" It may be that our answer would be an immediate, "Yes, of course it will". But there would be an uneasy feeling that we were acquiescing in a wrong attitude towards the positive ministry of healing which we believe the Church to have.

Might we not be perpetuating the idea that the ministry of healing meant no more than "at the best a vague but

unhopeful expectation of some ill-defined benefit which
might accompany the giving of the sacraments, as if they
were a kind of ecclesiastical placebo or tonic"? Indeed, Dr
Lambourne goes on to speculate that "in fact these administrations, like their medical equivalents, perhaps owed their
popularity to the relief from the sense of uselessness which
came to ministers, with the feeling that they were doing
something positive, getting on with something in the face of
chronic sickness".

Let us beware, then, of an excessively individualistic approach to the sacraments. When we prepare Mr Jones for
"sick communion", let us remind him that he is to take part
in a corporate act of the whole Church, that Christ comes to
heal both body and soul in every act of Communion, and
that this is the routine preventive and healing sacrament of
the Church, for the maintenance and restoration of health.

And when healing has come, the priest has no more right
to say, "Look what I have done through the sacraments"
than the doctor has the right to say, "Look what I have done
by my medicine or my surgery". We must say, "Look what
God has done through the sacraments of healing and the
skills and techniques of the doctor", just as the humble surgeon will say, "I performed an operation but it was God (or
the wonderful healing powers of nature) who wrought the
cure."

THE ADMINISTRATION OF
HOLY COMMUNION

In many parishes, of course, Communion will be given to sick
people only when the whole of the service provided in the
Book of Common Prayer has been used. This practice has
much to be said for it in cases of chronic illness when the
patient is never able to be present at a celebration of the
Eucharist in church. A portable altar is advisable, or if that
is not possible, a small table should be prepared with a
white cloth, cross, and candlesticks, a small bowl of water
and some flowers. Let the celebration of the "most

comfortable sacrament" be done with brightness and joy and thanksgiving. Let the friends and relatives and neighbours be present and receive communion with the sick one.

It is important in regard to this and all other sacramental administrations that the patient should know what is going on. The service should be simple and uncomplicated: there should be no need for the patient to turn from one place in his prayer book or leaflet to another. Anything printed should be in fairly large type, and there should be no abstruse rubrics to engage the attention or interest of the communicant during the service.

"The Body of our Lord Jesus Christ which was given for thee, preserve thy *body and soul* unto everlasting life."

COMMUNION FROM THE RESERVED SACRAMENT

This form of administration is much shorter and much more practicable in the case of someone who is seriously ill or unable to concentrate on any service longer than seven or eight minutes. Some clergy will prefer to make use of what is called "extended communion" which would seem to mean temporary as opposed to perpetual reservation. In other churches there is perpetual reservation, and the consecrated species are reserved, sometimes in both kinds, sometimes by intinction (i.e. touching the edge or centre of the wafer with a drop of the consecrated wine), and sometimes in one kind. Whatever our practice is, our duty as guardians of the sacraments is clear—we should make every effort to ensure the safety and reverent treatment of the sacred elements in church or hospital. The aumbries or safes or tabernacles should be kept locked; the vessels in which we reserve or carry the Sacrament should be kept scrupulously clean; the purificators or linen that we use should be washed regularly; our clothing and demeanour when we are carrying the Sacrament to the sick should be appropriate and dignified.

One is often asked, "When you are carrying the Sacrament to the sick, ought you to speak to people?" Our answer is "Yes, if the people you meet are not likely to understand what you are doing", and the remarks of Father Geoffrey Beaumont haunt the mind: "I am sure that with the Blessed Sacrament one ought always to be polite. . . . Our Lord would have been . . . which is a thing which people often do forget when they are taking the Sacrament through the streets."

Perhaps the most important duty we have to perform in regard to Communion of the Sick is that of instructing our communicants beforehand about what they are going to do. Many people are bewildered if the priest arrives at a bedside, either at home or in a hospital ward, and begins the service without any indication of what form the administration is to take, and at which point they are to receive the Sacrament, and how they are to receive it. Communicants should be given a card or leaflet beforehand to study, and opportunity must be given for them to ask any questions; above all, they must be put at ease. If the patient is too ill to read, then quiet, verbal instruction should be given.

It need hardly be said that punctuality is a necessary—and courteous factor. There will have been a great effort to see that the patient has been made comfortable and the room prepared; if he is in hospital, it may be that ward routine has been adjusted so that our visit may be made when the ward is quiet. We must see that we are similarly considerate in regard to the way we obey the clock.

Many parishes have "sick communion boxes" which contain the linen, cross, and candlesticks, cruets and other things necessary for the administration. These are taken to the house beforehand and collected afterwards. It is possible for a group of lay helpers to be responsible for the care and distribution of these boxes; in some cases, it will be possible for them to be present at the actual administration.

THE SACRAMENT OF UNCTION

"Ah, this is where you are beginning to talk about the ministry of healing" some readers might say. As if true healing consisted only of "cures" effected by slightly abstruse or unusual ministrations. But what we have tried to maintain in this book is that all true healing is sacramental, concerned with the whole man and the whole man linked to heaven, and that healing which comes through visitation of the priest, through ministry of doctor or nurse, or by therapeutic care of community, is, in the eyes of the Church, always an act of conversion towards Jesus.

Anointing means the bringing of ease of mind and body to a sick person by the scripturally appointed way, but it is also a form of ordination to the ministry of suffering by which the individual shares in the redemptive work of Christ in his Church.

But what does all this mean for us in our ministerial care of Mr Jones? We shall not regard this sacrament as something to be used in the last resort—when everything else has "failed"—or as a sacrament to be administered only when he is on his death-bed, but as a means of bringing to him life and wholeness and forgiveness in Christ.

This is not to say that there will not be many occasions when we shall feel that, faced with a dying or unconscious patient, we can do no other than administer the sacrament of holy unction—it will be the only objective, concrete, scriptural form of ministry we can perform for the body and soul of the dying person.

Lastly, we need to remember, as Dom Robert Petitpierre has reminded us, that "as in the Sacramentary of Serapion the oil for frying pancakes is blessed with almost the same prayer as the oil for anointing the sick, so with a particular patient the laying on of hands or receiving of Unction is no more important than their moral life, their surrender to God, their practice of prayer, their kindness to their neighbours, their duty to their families".

PRACTICAL DETAILS

The oil should be of the best vegetable kind, should be kept in a stock, such as is available at most church-furnishing firms. It should be renewed once a year—in most dioceses oil is blessed at a central service on Maundy Thursday. In the house where the sacrament is to be administered there should be cotton wool ready as well as bread crumbs for cleansing the fingers, in addition to the arrangements usually made for the normal Sick Communion.

THE LAYING-ON OF HANDS

Just as the physician, surgeon, nurse, masseur use their hands in their ministry to the sick, so should the priest. His handshake, his holding of hands, his giving of a blessing at the end of a visit are all "sacramentals" and can bring comfort and strength. The longer and more formal service of the Laying-on of Hands, referred to in the Bibliography, might be used during a church service, such as the Parish Communion or at a service when the whole work of the local hospitals is being laid before God.

To quote again from Dom Robert Petitpierre: "Unction, prayer, blessings, the laying on of hands, can, like Confession, only be fruitful, only have meaning if they lead the soul by a willed and joyful act back to Jesus Christ the Lord. We must not let folk fall into the trap of thinking that Jesus exists to do us good."

THE SACRAMENT OF PENANCE

This, again, is a sacrament of healing. Of course we recoil from the idea that illness of any kind is something sent by God to punish those who have disobeyed his commands, but of course we believe that there is an inalienable connection between sin and suffering. The pathologist will tell us how bad temper and disloyalty, for instance, will lead to changes in gland secretions which may bring about physical ailments.

But it will not be our duty as parish pastors to speculate on the causes of Mr Jones's ailments (spiritually speaking or psycho-somatically speaking), but to lead him to penitence and reparation. In the majority of cases there will be no formal confession. Many people will open their hearts to us and it will be our duty to listen patiently and sympathetically. At the end, they may say, "Well, don't you think I'm awful?" and we can say "No—and God doesn't. You *are* sorry, aren't you, for what you've done wrong. I'll say a prayer asking for God's forgiveness."

This is not formal absolution and we should not give the impression that it is, but we are persuaded that this is the beginning of the way back for many ordinary church people. Most people have never received any instruction about penance, most people think that it is a Roman Catholic practice and they know all the popular arguments against it. (Mrs O'Hara next door goes to confession every Saturday night, then comes home drunk and keeps the whole street awake.)

But the priest will find in his ministry to the sick that there will be many occasions when Mr Jones or someone like him will say, "Look, Vicar, there's been something on my conscience for a long time and I'd like to get it off my chest." That is the time when we can gently instruct him about the sacrament of penance. There will be many occasions when a person who knows that he is dying will seek the priest's absolving ministry. *We ought to know what to do.*

It is not the purpose of this volume to treat in detail the theory and practice of penance, nor would the author be competent to deal with this subject. He must refer the reader to the literature on the subject. But there are a few points which are especially relevant to our ministry to the sick which might be stressed. These points are based on a conversation with the Reverend F. E. P. Langton.

1. We are priests ministering the salvation which our Lord has won for us, and we must therefore regard the Seal of the Confessional most strictly. We may be trying to co-operate with doctors or psychiatrists, and there can be a danger that in discussing a case we might, in order to be helpful (or to appear knowledgeable), reveal something we have heard in confession. We must be very careful about this.

2. When a person is sick and weary it may not be possible for the "material" integrity of his or her confession to be complete. Very often people find it difficult to find the appropriate word for their sin, and we must be very gentle and patient. It is good to have a simple form of self-examination based on the Ten Commandments or the Beatitudes which we can use for questioning. Then the patient need only answer Yes or No or indicate this by pressure of the hand (if in the sight of others) or by nodding or shaking of the head if speech is impossible.

3. Scrupulous people (i.e. people who can never be convinced that God has forgiven them *all* their sins) will most probably engage our attention. It is easy to lose patience with such people, who many experts in spiritual direction would claim are invariably neurotic cases. Gentleness combined with firmness should be used; and often, though not always, psychiatric treatment should be recommended.

THE SACRAMENT OF HOLY BAPTISM

There will be many occasions on which the priest will be called to baptize children in emergency. When babies are born prematurely they are placed in an incubator and baptism is effected with a small spoon. Most maternity wards have a "christening set" in which there is a small font, cross, and candlesticks, baptismal shell or spoon, and stole. The usual form of service consists of the Lord's Prayer, the Blessing of the Water, the Baptism (without the form of reception into the Church) and a prayer of thanksgiving and the Blessing.

The parents should be told how the baby should be brought to church when it recovers, so that the whole of the Baptism Service may be held, with god-parents present (missing out, of course, the actual Baptism).

There will be other occasions when sick people desire baptism. Sometimes it is possible to have the whole of the service; when a person is dying and unable to follow a long service, it may be shortened as with babies.

Although we do not, like the Roman Catholic priests, have the delegated power to confirm patients, it will quite often be our privilege to ask a bishop to perform the Laying-on of Hands at a sick parishioner's bed-side. So often people think that it is too late in life to have their baptism completed in this way, but with a little effort on the part of everybody, this "unusual" administration can be arranged. One cannot but recall the joy that came to one patient of ninety years —and the edification brought to the rest of the ward—by the visit of Bishop Mervyn Stockwood to confirm a dying patient. *It did us all good.*

And so the wheel has come full circle. Because "Baptism is the first great sacrament of healing. By his baptism the sick man is already a member of the regenerated creation and the healing church. It is only required that he should of his own free will appropriate the free gifts of healing earned by Christ for him. Because Baptism joins man to Christ, man participates both actively and passively in the regenerative and healing work of Christ. He is joined to a therapeutic community in which the members both heal and receive healing. He is admitted as a healer and one in need of being healed."[1]

[1] R. A. Lambourne, op. cit.

Bibliography

A Priest's Work in Hospital, edited by J. G. Cox (S.P.C.K.)
A manual published under the auspices of the Church of England Hospital Chaplains' Fellowship some years ago. The volume has some useful illustrations.

Order for the Administration of Holy Communion (S.P.C.K.)
This is available on cards or in pamphlet form and is widely used in hospitals and sick rooms.

Order for the Administration of Holy Unction and the Laying on of Hands (S.P.C.K.)
On 6 June 1935 the Upper House of the Convocation of Canterbury agreed to the following motion: "That this house gives approval to the Service for Unction and the Laying-on of Hands without Unction for provisional use in the Province subject to due diocesan sanction."

Community, Church and Healing, by R. A. Lambourne (Darton, Longman and Todd)
A recent (1963) radical study in the theology of the Church's whole mission of healing.

Notes for the Guidance of the Part-time Hospital Chaplain (C.I.O. for the Hospital Chaplaincies Council of the Church Assembly)
Useful summary of the hospital set-up and of the chaplain's duties together with some useful addresses.

To the Anglican Nurse (C.I.O.)
A leaflet designed for the probationer nurse to help her to help the visiting priest or minister.

The Pastoral Care of the Mentally Ill, by Norman Autton (S.P.C.K.)
A comprehensive study of the priest's work in dealing with patients at home or in hospital who are suffering from mental disorder.

Ordeal of Wonder, by Bishop E. R. Morgan (O.U.P.)
A theological inquiry written for all those "who believe that theology matters to the ministry of healing" and for the priest or doctor who is trying to reach mutual understanding in this field.

Report of the Archbishops' Commission on the Church's Ministry of Healing (S.P.C.K.)

Called to serve, by Paul Gliddon and Muriel Powell (Hodder and Stoughton)
A book for all who care for the sick, who face the problem of suffering and seek a right sense of vocation.

Ministering to the Physically Sick, by Carl J. Scherzer (Prentice-Hall)
An American manual of practical pastoralia for the sick-room. This volume has been of inestimable help to the author of *Sick Call*.

How to make your Confession, by P. D. Butterfield (S.P.C.K.)
A primer for members of the Church of England.

A Guide for Spiritual Directors, by the author of *The Way* (Mowbray)

The Priest's Vade Mecum, edited by T. W. Crafer (S.P.C.K.)
A valuable source of prayers to be incorporated in the priest's personal armoury of prayers and devotions for his own ministry to the sick.

Psychiatry Today, by David Stafford Clark (Pelican)
The author of this book has given invaluable help to priests at Chaplains' Training Courses and Conferences.

The Priest and Penance, by Kenneth Mackenzie (Mowbray)
A very simple guide to the hearing of confessions.

I was sick and ye visited me, by M. M. Martin (Faith Press)
A book on sick visiting by a priest of great experience.

Holy Unction—a Practical Guide, by Henry Cooper (Guild of St Raphael)

Your Suffering, by Maurice Wood (Hodder and Stoughton)

Some Moral Problems, by Thomas Wood (S.P.C.K.)

An English Benedictional, by Richard Tatlock (Faith Press)
A fascinating quarry for blessings to be given to sick people.